C000085336

Achieving Balance

A simple book that will change your life

Warm Regards,

Allan Willis

Allan Phillip x

manicboy publishing

Achieving Balance: A simple book that will change your life

Published 2012

Email: allan.willis@achieving-balance.co.uk
Website: www.achieving-balance.co.uk
Facebook: www.facebook.com/achieving-balance
Twitter: www.twitter.com/AchievesBalance

Disclaimer: The information provided in this book represents the thoughts and opinions of the author and should not be construed as personal medical advice or instruction. No action should be taken solely based on the contents of this book. Readers should consult professional health practitioners for any matter relating to their health and well-being. The text is presented in good faith and the author does not accept any liability for any errors or omissions. Readers who fail to consult the appropriate health authorities do so at their own risk.

ISBN 978-0-9573069-0-5
Illustrations Carien Yatsiv
Typeset in Minion
Printed in Great Britain by LDI Print, New Yatt, Witney, Oxon
Cover, typesetting and interior design Clockwork Graphic Design

To my amazing wife Gill

Thank you for your love and support through the
good times and the bad.

To my very special children George and Nathalie

Thank you for showing me what matters in life.

To my Mum and Dad, Lionel and Hanne

Thank you for teaching me to always seek the truth.

To my brother Ralph

Thank you for the time we have spent together.

To Phyllis and Ron

Thank you for your support over the years.

Acknowledgements

Special thanks to the following people for their help in the making of this book:

Carien Yatsiv, Artist
For her amazing illustrations.
www.carienyatsiv.com

Sarah Williams, The Book Consultancy
For her invaluable help with editing and compiling the text.
www.thebookconsultancy.com

Jane Bigos
For her brilliant work on the graphic design and layout.
www.clockworkgraphicdesign.co.uk

Debra Clark
For her fantastic support and unwavering faith in the book.
www.darlingbudsphotography.com

Emily and Harry Wallace
For inspiring me to write the book I had been thinking about for many years and for being a great photographer.

John Rawcliffe
For being a true friend.
www.bluewhalewebdesign.co.uk/

Andrew Taylor, **Andy Evans** and **David Lilley**
www.bigbootclub.co.uk
For your wisdom over the years.

To my great friends with whom I have had fantastic times:
Andy N, Jim G, Garth H, Andy D, David W, Louise W, Harry W, Hamish W, Nicky D, Alan D, Diarmuid L, Mags L, Mark L, Janet L, Mark Von H, Marc A, Nina, Sam F, Jean Michel J, Rob L, Andy K, Cynthia K, Malcolm K, Janet K, Stan B, Anne B, Graeme B, Miles P, Sangita S, Dominic E, Michelle W, Sarah G, Tony K, Helen S, Sue E, Heidi L, Diana T, Thorsten J, Jean D, Janet A, Bobby E, Gianni M, Jeff D, Patricia W, Micahel T, Mike S, Tia, Linda M, Gary M, Victor T, Tracy T, Lucy, Paul M, Gina M, Debbie H-S, Martin H-S, Rupert H, Richard T, Paul J, Jason C, Andy M and special thoughts to those who are no longer with us.

Introduction

Balance affects all of us, each and every person on the planet, without exception.

It affects the quality of our decision making, the way that we view the world and ultimately the quality of our lives and those around us.

There are several elements that constitute balance but once you understand them there are several ways to make small changes that have a positive effect on your life.

Achieving Balance is not the sole preserve of spiritual masters, gurus and the like. The things they are doing can be done by anyone who has a certain level of knowledge and a resolve to apply some of the techniques to their life.

No-one has a genetic reason why they cannot find balance. It is a choice of the individual.

The only pre-requisite is an open mind!

If you think of balance as like trying to juggle several balls in the air simultaneously then it can be seen that knowing what the individual balls are is essential to actually achieving balance.

The reality is that during the course of our lives some of us get closer than others to understanding and applying balance to our lives.

That said, achieving balance and fulfilment is open to all of us. How do I know that? Because fulfilment and balance are not dependent on external factors, they are only dependent on the perspective you choose to adopt.

You are unique and the balance that you feel is a measure of the degree to which your self-image is aligned to who you really are. Often people have a self-image that is out of line with who they really are and this leads to a feeling of internal conflict, low self-esteem and poor balance.

The universe simply is, and your choice is how much you want to love it. If you learn to love your existence in every moment then you will have found the Holy Grail and Nirvana of balance. True fulfilment.

This book will help you get closer to that state of mind.

Balance is a big subject but it doesn't have to be complicated, although it is often made out to be unduly complex.

For many years I have had a passion for balance, an interest in finding answers to the question 'How do I achieve balance and fulfilment in my life?' This quest has involved reading literally hundreds of books and contemplating several of the philosophical questions that pop up along the way.

My experience is that sometimes you have to read books the size of an encyclopedia to find that nugget of information, the next piece of the jigsaw that you have been searching for.

But it doesn't have to be that way.

One day it occurred to me that any idea can be expressed as a page, a paragraph and a picture. This is the core essence of any idea or concept. The core essence of a 350 page book can be explained in a page. Eureka!

And so, Achieving Balance was born.

A book designed to explain often difficult concepts in a way that is accessible and digestible to the reader whilst giving them an understanding of the main concepts of balance and how to apply them to their life.

The first half of the book is designed to give an overview of the main concepts and aspects of balance.

The second half of the book helps you understand how to practically apply balance to your life. This is done in 'bite size' chunks to make the changes easier to understand and apply.

The book will give you everything that has taken me the last twenty-five years of my life to discover. I wish I could have read the book myself twenty-five years ago!

Furthermore, I have recommended some books that I have found to be useful, that will help you expand your knowledge on the various topics.

You will discover in the book that you are part of me as much as I am part of you. We are all connected and are part of the same thing at the end of the day. So I sincerely wish you a pleasant journey through the world of balance and I hope you find the balance and fulfilment that you seek and that all of us crave.

Bon Voyage!

Part One:
What is Balance?

Contents

Part One: What is Balance?

1 The Emotional Rollercoaster

Life has many ups and downs and it can sometimes feel like being on an emotional rollercoaster.

This can be exhausting and emotionally draining and can contribute to a lack of balance and wellbeing. The question is 'what is causing us to feel this way?' and, moreover, 'what can we do to improve the way we are feeling?'

Let us first look at the ingredients that cause disappointments in our life. It is not the event we experience itself that causes us to be disappointed but instead it is our expectation of how the event is going to be that is the culprit.

In a nutshell, disappointment is the difference between our expectation of an event and the way it actually turns out to be. Think about if you were going to a party and you thought it was going to be a great night out and when you got there you were the only person there. You would be disappointed because the expectation was that it was going to be great and the reality was that it wasn't great. The difference between the expectation and the reality created the disappointment, not the event itself.

Every day people have several expectations of the events in the day ahead and inevitably when the reality of the events is different to the expectation this creates a series of disappointments. Of course the opposite could happen if the reality is better than the expectation - this will create an emotional high.

Some of our expectations are thought about in our conscious mind and others are reflex expectations that are embedded in our subconscious mind. It is like when you go to the dentist and subconsciously you expect it to be a painful and unpleasant experience. You don't have to think about it because your expectation of the event is generated automatically.

So it can be seen that our expectations of events are the key factors that lead to disappointments and emotional highs and drive the emotional rollercoaster that we experience.

The question is how do we turn the rollercoaster white-knuckle ride into a calm, relaxing and balanced journey through our lives?

The answer is to always have an expectation that events will be as they are going to be. If you look at events in this way it follows that when the reality of the event turns out to be as it is, this is always the same as your expectation. This means that you do not experience disappointment or emotional highs because events are always in line with your expectations and you have freed yourself from the emotional rollercoaster.

Changing your expectations is another way of saying that you are accepting events as they are as opposed to having an expectation that they are going to be how you want them to be. If you think about it, the only thing you control is what you do or what you think and so it would be unreasonable to expect everything to happen in the way you want it to, given the number of things that are outside your control.

This seemingly simple concept is a key element in emotional balance and understanding and applying this principle is very important.

> *To free yourself from the emotional rollercoaster, have an expectation that events will be as they are going to be. Learn to accept things the way they are and do not expect events to be how you want them to be.*

2 Respect of Boundaries

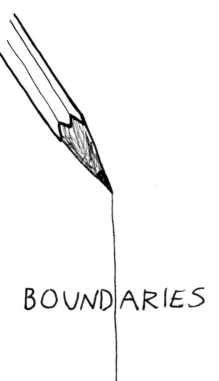

BOUNDARIES

Interactions with other people, from transient encounters to long term relationships, are governed by a set of rules defined by a person. These rules take the form of boundaries that define how the interaction is going to take place. Boundaries are like a set of permissions and gates that dictate what is allowed and what isn't.

The boundaries that a person has will vary depending on the person that they are interacting with.

How someone behaves around their boss at work is likely to be very different to how they would behave with their best friend. The boundaries with the boss are likely to be greater than the more relaxed boundaries around the best friend.

When two people get together there are two main processes taking place. There is the projection of your own boundaries and the picking up of the boundaries of the other person. These processes can sometimes take place at the time of the meeting or they are often established early on in a friendship and these ground rules are applied by default during the course of the friendship or until something changes.

So how do these boundaries affect personal balance? The fact is that if your personal boundaries are violated it can lead to feelings of low self worth, anger and depression. If you violate other people's boundaries then it affects your own balance as well.

In a perfect world all personal interactions would be mutually consensual. That is to say that people would always take the trouble to establish where your boundaries are and respect them and you would do the same for them. But it doesn't always work that way in practice. Why is that?

Well, there are a number of reasons boundaries are violated. The first reason is that someone is not projecting or asserting their boundaries. They may not realise what feels comfortable for them. It is quite common, if someone has an overdeveloped fear of authority, that they feel unable to assert a boundary to, say, a senior person at work. Or sometimes they just feel uncomfortable saying no to someone.

The second reason is that the person someone is interacting with either doesn't pick up the boundaries or chooses to ignore them anyway. The social antenna to pick up boundaries is developed to different degrees in different people and ignoring boundaries is often related to control issues.

It should be remembered that communication of boundaries can be verbal but is often more subtle with body language or facial expression.

You will never achieve balance in your self if your boundaries are being violated or you are violating other people's boundaries.

Think about the relationships and interactions in your life and ask yourself whether you need to define your boundaries and assert them more effectively, or whether you need to respect other people's boundaries more effectively, or both.

Once you recognise what is happening with respect to the boundaries in your life then you need to apply changes to become more or less assertive.

> *You will never achieve balance in your self if your boundaries are being violated or you are violating other people's boundaries.*

3   Self Reference and Object Reference

People's behaviour is often driven by the need to please others or to conform to the latest fashion or peer group pressure. In a nutshell, most people do not want to be the odd one out or different from everyone else.

This type of behaviour is known as 'object reference', which is the need to seek external reference or approval for one's actions or behaviour.

The pressure to conform can come directly or through advertising or latterly through social networks which act as a kind of amplifier for peer pressure. Fashion is a subtle form of object reference where people feel the need to dress the same way.

The problem with object reference is that the way you are expected to behave will vary depending on who you are with. This means that you have to develop multiple personalities which can become emotionally exhausting and difficult to keep track of.

Object reference can also become destructive when you try to imitate a celebrity whose image has been airbrushed. This can lead to eating disorders, trying to achieve a body shape that is unachievable. The emphasis on celebrity culture in recent years has made this type of fixation all the more commonplace.

The opposite to object reference is self-reference. This is when behaviour and actions are decided by reference to one's self or personal compass as opposed to any external influence. The advantage is that no matter what situation is encountered a person will always behave in a consistent way that is true to who they are and to their sense of self. There is only room for a single personality, which is emotionally less exhausting than multiple personalities.

Self-reference is a more sustainable way of behaving than object reference and is a key component of achieving balance. If your behaviour is driven by external factors out of your control, through object reference, then you will never find balance.

Self-reference is another way of saying self belief or the extent to which you have confidence in your own judgement. It should be remembered that you cannot please everyone. Learn to accept it. Don't waste time with the people you are never going to please.

Think about your day to day life and ask yourself the question 'How much of what I do is conforming to or pleasing others and how much is what I really want to do?'

To achieve balance adjust your behaviour and actions to always be true to who you are. Your values will form the foundation of your behaviour and you need to be clear as to what your values are and be true to them.

If people cannot accept you for who you are as opposed to how they want you to be then they are having a negative impact on your balance and are best removed from your list of associates.

> *Self reference is a more sustainable way of behaving than object reference and is a key component to achieving balance.*
>
> *To achieve balance adjust your behaviour and actions to always be true to who you are and be clear and consistent about your values.*

4 Change and Uncertainty

A paradox that we all have to come to terms with is that the only constant in our lives is change. It stands to reason that if someone is unable to accept the change and uncertainty in their life then they will not be able to achieve balance.

The ability to predict events that are uncertain and to adapt to change are the key concepts behind evolutionary success.

So why do people find it hard to accept uncertainty and change?

Most people have a deep craving for security and certainty, the desire to know that everything will be OK, that everyone around them will be safe, that things will stay as they are.

This desire for certainty manifests itself in the form of fear which is an emotion that underpins behaviours such as control issues, jealousy, overprotective parenting and money hoarding to name but a few.

At the heart of these behaviours is the desire to control the outcomes of the events in one's life.

Unfortunately, because a person can only control their own thoughts and actions, they are constantly fighting a battle that cannot be won. The universe is going to do what it wants at any particular time and it is constantly changing. Whichever way you look at it, attempting to control the universe to behave in a way that is more certain for you is impossible. You can load the odds slightly more in your favour for a favourable outcome by choosing the best actions, but you can never control events.

So how can we learn to accept change and uncertainty?

A starting point would be to consider what would happen if you lived in a world that was certain and there was no change. It would be a bit like being King Midas when he was able to turn everything to gold - after a short time controlling everything would become very boring because nothing would ever happen that you weren't expecting! If you think about your life, it is the fact that everything is uncertain that makes life interesting and gives you a reason to wake up in the morning.

The reality is that you live in a world that is always changing through factors that are outside your control. The universe is massively bigger than you are and trying to control it will have a negative impact on your mental and physical balance.

So maybe it is time to wave the white flag of surrender, to accept that your life is based on change and uncertainty, to embrace it and learn to love it and to accept it. The universe isn't going to change the way it works, so maybe it is time you make the changes.

Learn to accept things how they are and not how you want them to be. Heard that before!?

> *The reality is that you live in a world that is uncertain and is always changing through factors that are outside of your control. The universe is massively bigger than you are and trying to control it will have a negative impact on your balance.*

5 The Love Triangle

If you had to distill the secret to balance and fulfilment into its core essence, in its simplest form, then the love triangle would be the answer.

So what is the love triangle?

> ***Love yourself unconditionally***
> ***Love yourself for who you are and not for who or***
> ***what you wish you were.***

How many times do people think if only I lost some weight, if I had some plastic surgery, if I had more money then I would love myself more? These are thoughts that constantly drain people emotionally and cause poor balance.

People may have come to believe the criticisms of others, have been made to feel a failure in childhood, or simply feel pressured to be like a role model or celebrity.

Isn't it time to cut yourself some slack?

The limit of the love that you have for yourself is the limit of the love that you can give, so attaching conditions to your self love will also affect those people around you.

Unless you learn to accept yourself for who you are, warts and all, by loving yourself unconditionally then you will never achieve true balance.

> ***Love others unconditionally***
> ***Love others for who they are and not for who or***
> ***what you would like them to be.***

For many people the amount of love they have for others is dependent on a set of conditions and is therefore conditional love.

People are often judgemental when they meet people, sometimes consciously and sometimes subconsciously. What does someone look like? What colour is their skin? What are they wearing? And what do they do for a living?

These questions act as a kind of filter to determine the degree to which you love that person.

In a spiritual context, which we will examine in another section, we are all connected and by filtering out people you think you don't like by imposing conditional love on them you are in effect shooting yourself in the foot and adversely affecting your own balance.

Everyone on this earth is doing you a favour, and should be loved for it, by either setting you an example of what to do or setting an example of what not to do. Both examples are valuable to you and it is important to appreciate this in others. It is like they are all characters in your life and need to be respected for their respective roles.

Unless you learn to love others without imposing conditions then you will not achieve balance.

> ***Love what is unconditionally***
> ***Love what is for what it is and not for what you***
> ***wish it was.***

If only it wasn't raining, if my house was bigger, if I had a new car, if my boyfriend hadn't just left me. A familiar story?

These are all conditions that are imposed on the moment of time being experienced to determine how much that moment is being loved.

True balance and happiness is experienced when each and every moment is loved.

This can only be possible when no conditions are attached to how much you love any particular moment. If you impose conditions and most things in the universe are outside of your control then it follows that you will not love what is happening to you.

The universe is exactly as it is meant to be at any given moment. Accept what is. Accept each and every moment. Learn to love each moment without spoiling it by imposing conditions on whether you love it or not.

Balance can only be achieved by Loving What Is.

> *The secret to balance and fulfilment is to*
> *Love yourself unconditionally*
> *Love others unconditionally*
> *Love what is unconditionally*
> *Simple words that take a lifetime to master.*

6   The Ocean and the Drop

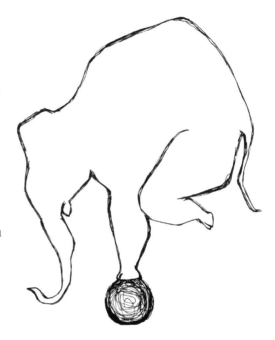

The ocean and the drop is a simple analogy but it is fundamental to achieving balance.

It hinges around the way that you perceive yourself (the individual) and everything that is around you (the collective).

It would be fair to say that most people see themselves as a distinct person who is separate and unconnected to everything that is around them. This view of life is known as a dualistic ego perspective. The perspective is dualistic because it implies that you and the rest of the universe are two separate and distinct things. The ego is the sense that a person has of being a separate entity or a separate individual.

The fuel of the ego is fear.

So what is wrong with someone seeing themselves as an individual?

In short there is nothing wrong with this view but to achieve balance someone must understand the exact opposite perspective to this, the holistic view.

Let us first imagine that the universe is like a vast ocean of energy. Einstein told us that E=mc2, which means that matter is actually only a different form of energy. So in effect everything, including you, is merely energy in different forms! Please excuse the physics but it is the best way to explain the ocean and the drop.

So it turns out that you are actually a little squiggle or drop of energy, in a vast ocean of energy that is known as the universe.

If you imagine a drop of water in an ocean, and then ask the question 'Is the drop a separate drop of water or is it just a small and integral part of the whole ocean?' The answer to this would be that both statements are true and it would depend on how you were looking at it.

The separate drop is the equivalent of the dualistic ego perspective.

Seeing yourself as being a small part of the whole ocean is a holistic perspective. This is where you consider yourself to be an integral part of the collective. With this view you are connected to everything around you and are part of the whole. You are not a separate entity.

Imagine your ego to be like a lens that zooms in and out. If the lens is zoomed in then you see yourself as a separate entity (100% ego state) and if it is zoomed out then you see yourself as part of the whole (0% ego state).

It can be seen that if your zoom lens is not working very well because it is locked in an ego perspective then this will cause poor decision making and consequently affect your balance.

It also turns out that the degree to which you zoom in and out of your ego state affects your perception of time. If you are absorbed in something and zoomed in then time appears to pass more quickly and if you are zoomed out in a meditative state then time appears to run more slowly. How long you live for, or at least appear to live for, will depend on your perception! So if you want to live longer start meditating.

> *So it turns out that you are actually a little squiggle or drop of energy, in a vast ocean of energy that is known as the universe. You can either see yourself as separate to the ocean or as an integral part of the whole ocean. Achieving balance involves understanding both viewpoints.*

7 Interdependence is a higher value than Independence and Dependence

Interdependence is when someone is mutually and physically responsible to others and shares a common set of principles with them, but at the same time is self-reliant emotionally, economically and morally.

Independence is when someone is completely self-contained and is responsible for themselves only.

Dependence is when someone cannot survive or exist in a relationship without the other person.

Stephen Covey, author of *The 7 Habits of Highly Effective People*, put forward an order of emotional maturity with interdependence as being a higher value than independence which is a higher value than dependence.

This order of emotional maturity could also be used as a barometer for a person's capability to achieve balance. An understanding and application of interdependence will lead to balance, while dependence will lead to imbalance.

There are parallels with the ocean and the drop analogy. The drop, or ego, separate entity perspective equates to independence whilst the ocean holistic perspective equates to interdependence where everything is interconnected and mutually responsible.

The ocean perspective is therefore a higher value than the drop perspective.

The principles of interdependence are in some respects the same as those of spirituality. In spirituality there is a sense of connectedness with a larger reality and with interdependence there is a sense of connectedness and mutual responsibility for others and indeed everything.

An example of interdependence is the 'green' movement where people have got together with a mutual desire to preserve the environment as they realise there is a common interest to do so.

To achieve balance you must first of all understand where you are on the emotional maturity journey from the lowest value of dependence to the highest of interdependence.

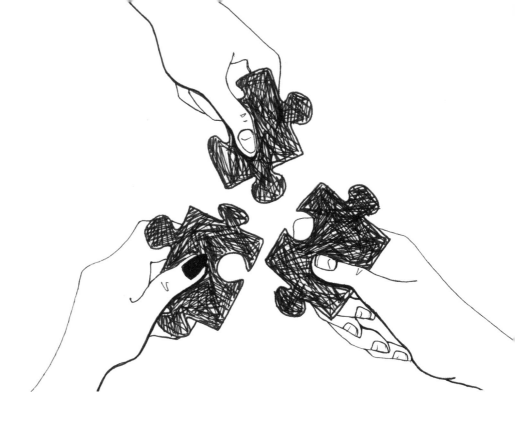

It is important to recognise that no-one is an island and achieving balance is about acting in a way that is in the interests of the collective or the ocean whilst at the same time being in the best interests of the individual or the drop.

Behaviour that is interdependent is always seeking to find the 'win-win' action or response at any given time.

Most people tend to behave in a way that is skewed to their own self-interest and this leads to a lack of emotional balance.

> *It is important to recognise that no-one is an island and achieving balance is about acting in a way that is in the interests of the collective or the ocean whilst at the same time being in the best interests of the individual or the drop. This is known as the win–win scenario.*

8   The Engine Driver and the Passenger

The question I am going to ask you is that if your life was like a train then would you be the engine driver in control of what happens to you or would you simply be a passenger who just accepts what happens to you without any control over the events in your life?

I would guess that you would say that you are the engine driver as ordinary logic would tell you that you are in control of your own actions.

For an explanation let us go back to the analogy of the ocean and the drop. The question is:

> *Is it the drop that decides where it moves or is it the forces acting on the drop from the ocean that determines the motion of the drop?*

The answer to this question is that both things are true and it would depend if you were looking from the perspective of the drop or from the perspective of the ocean.

Common sense would suggest that given that the ocean is far larger than the drop that it would control the motion of the drop.

People's lives behave in much the same way. As discussed earlier, people are like a drop of energy in an ocean of energy that we call the universe. So if you were looking from the perspective of the universe it could be argued that it was the forces of the universe acting on a person that was causing the events in that person's life. However from the person's perspective it appears that they were controlling the events in their life. As an example, if you were to lift up your hand then is it you doing it or is it the forces acting upon you from the universe? Both ways it would feel the same and so it would just depend on how you were looking at it. Think about those old Hollywood movies where someone is driving a car that is obviously static in the studio and the background is moving to create the appearance of motion. The same question can be asked 'Is it the car moving or is it the scenery?' Is it the universe moving or is it you? As Einstein pointed out in his paper on relativity, it is the relative motion that is the important thing.

The universe could be static and you are moving or you could be static and the universe is moving; either way it would feel the same.

This creates the paradox that a person is both the engine driver and the passenger in their life at the same time. This seeming coexistence of opposites is possible because events can be viewed from different perspectives and both the ocean and drop are connected, which isn't immediately obvious.

This paradox has profound implications for the way your life can be viewed and for your ability to achieve balance.

Let us first consider what it means to be a passenger. In this scenario it is the forces of the universe acting upon us that decide what happens to us and we do not have any control over the events in our lives. If you consider the size of the universe relative to us then the idea of the universe controlling events is easy to visualise.

In this instance it follows that from the moment you are born until the moment you die events are predetermined and controlled by the universe. So how can you take responsibility for what happens? Because it was out of your control and was always going to happen anyway.

If you look at things in this way then it can be seen that the idea of guilt becomes unworkable. How can you feel guilty about something that was going to happen anyway and was outside your control?

Visualise the corkscrew ride at Alton Towers where the start represents your birth and the finish is your death. In the passenger view the universe decides what your unique ride is going to be for your life. You have no choice in the ride or the events that happen to you in your life. However this is a power-sharing deal between you and the universe, and you are given a choice on how you react to what happens to you on the ride, or the degree to which you enjoy or love the ride.

So you could go through the ride (your life) saying this is unfair, I wish this was different, I am worried about what happens in the future or alternatively you could accept the fact that you were a passenger and simply say I accept what is happening to me because it was going to happen anyway. In fact one end of the scale would be to say I love every moment of the ride and the other to say I hate (or 0% love) every moment of the ride. As with different people's lives, everyone's ride is different and the ride can be more extreme for some people than others.

When you start to understand the passenger view it can be quite liberating. It feels like the burdens of expectation, responsibility, guilt and fear are lifted from your shoulders and they are replaced with a feeling of acceptance that whatever happens to you was going to happen anyway. There is a feeling of accepting what actually is and not craving what you want events to be because the passenger realises that what is going to be is going to be, so why not learn how to enjoy it?

The engine driver view is, of course, the ego perspective. You see yourself as an individual who is in control of your own destiny. You take full responsibility for all your actions. This view can be quite exhausting as you always have to be alert to make sure everything is running OK. Meanwhile the passenger is relaxing in autopilot mode.

How is the engine driver going to feel at the end of the corkscrew ride, having been tense the whole way, only to find that the ride was going to happen that way anyway regardless of their input?

The universe has created the perfect system. You get the full experience of being the engine driver and being in control of your life but at the same time the controls have been disconnected without your knowledge and are in fact controlled by the universe. So the universe is like a driving instructor car with dual controls that can be used simultaneously, one set for it and one set for you and so everyone is happy.

The engine driver and the passenger analogy is another example of understanding different perspectives to create a more balanced view of life. For many people they almost fight against their life whereas with the passenger perspective they could flow naturally with their life.

Is it about time you became a passenger and learnt to enjoy events in your life more? They are going to happen anyway!

> *Your life is like the corkscrew ride at a theme park. The universe chooses the ride, which is different for all of us, and you choose how much you enjoy the ride. You can choose to look at it from the perspective of an engine driver or a passenger but either way it is going to happen anyway.*

9   Fear – the Ego's best friend

Fear is the fuel that enables the ego to exist.

A common theme so far in our exploration of balance has been the need to accept events that occur in your life. Fear is the emotion that underpins the non-acceptance of events and effectively puts a person into a tug of war or a lack of synchronicity with the universe. The universe is bigger than a person and inevitably the battle is a David and Goliath type contest which is exhausting emotionally, creates a lack of balance and is ultimately futile for an individual.

Fear takes a person away from the natural flow of things, makes life feel like hard work and spoils the enjoyment of life's journey.

The analogy of a fox trying to get into a farmyard to eat the chickens is a good way to describe fear. Fear is always there in a person's life, like the fox who is always prowling the perimeter fence of the farmyard, trying to gain access to their inner core to play an ever greater role in that person's life. It is only through being aware of fear and not allowing it to take over that people can lead balanced and fulfilled lives. If the fox comes into the farmyard then you need to be aware of it and drive it out before it can cause damage. Being more aware of fear makes it easier to balance it in your thoughts.

Too much fear is destructive in the same way that too little fear can be. If you didn't have a fear of putting your hand in a fire then there would be nothing to stop you burning yourself. This fear is a learned behaviour based on the experiences in your life.

So how can fear manifest itself?

There are many different forms of fear and associated behaviours that are underpinned by fear but they can broadly be described in three main forms.

The fear of your 'self', the fear of loss in relationships and of possessions, and the fear of events.

The fear of events can be in the past, present or future.

The fear of your 'self'

The fears surrounding your 'self', or put another way the non-acceptance of who you are, will manifest themselves in the form of a lack of self esteem, self confidence and self love.

This often leads to destructive behaviour patterns such as depression, self harm, OCD (Obsessive Compulsive Disorder) and addictions.

Some common substance addictions are alcoholism, drugs and painkillers. There are also behavioural addictions such as control issues and anorexia and physical addictions such as violence, exercise and sex

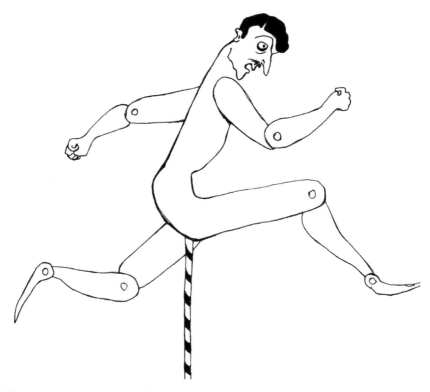

addiction. Pretty much anything can become an addiction if it forms a repetitive pattern and is destructive to the individual.

At the root of these behaviours there is always the lack of self acceptance or low self esteem which is fear based and is literally a fear of who you actually are.

Until someone can accept themselves for who they actually are (unconditional love) and not for who they feel they should be (conditional love) then they will never truly overcome their fears and achieve balance.

This is why true balance can only be found within, by accepting yourself. No matter how many drugs you take, how much alcohol you consume, how much money you accumulate you will never find balance and inner peace externally. Addicts are in effect running from themselves.

> *The long and winding road*
> *That leads to your door*
> *Will never disappear*
>
> McCartney & Lennon

The fear of loss of possessions

When people start out in life they often have nothing and therefore have nothing to lose.

As a result they tend to take more risk, or put another way, behave in a way that is less fearful. Time goes by and they accumulate money, possessions, pensions, insurances and so on and they develop a subconscious or conscious fear of losing what they have managed to accumulate.

This state of mind is known as attachment or the fear of loss.

The natural reaction is to ringfence what they already have and take less risk which can result in a 'rabbit in the headlights' form of paralysis. There is a vicious circle because as the amount that someone has increases the corresponding fear of losing it also increases. The fear of loss can become disproportionate in someone's life, which results in a loss of emotional balance and often a feeling of despair. This can lead to miserly behaviour, becoming a workaholic, obsessively watching share prices and so on.

How often have you heard someone close to retiring saying that they just need to work for another few years and then in a few years time they say the same thing? So what is going on?

There is an underlying fear that whatever they have is not quite enough and if they had a little bit more then this would be enough. When they have a little more they go through the same loop again. So there is always an underlying fear that they don't have enough. It is like chasing a carrot that keeps moving away from them every time they reach out to it. So, as it turns out, there is no absolute amount that is enough to live happily ever after and without fear.

> *The feeling of security that people strive after can never be found through external things such as money, power and possessions as there will always be the fear of loss.*

This feeling of security, the safe haven can only be found through acceptance or non fear of yourself, others and events. Becoming more aware of fear is a key part of managing it and achieving balance.

Fears are like the weeds in your garden. They are always there, they will always grow and they need to be recognised and managed but can never be eradicated. The more a person recognises the weeds, or put another way, the negative fear based emotions in their life, then the earlier they can be removed, which will result in less emotional damage and a greater feeling of balance.

The fear of loss in a relationship

The fear of loss in a relationship is a common problem and manifests itself in the behaviours such as control, jealousy and insecurity.

The picture is sometimes confused when someone might say that they are in love with someone when in actual fact they have an attachment to that person and a consequential fear of loss. The perceived love is actually dependency.

The controlling behaviours are all designed to enhance the feeling of certainty in the relationship but in actual fact they all create more uncertainty by driving their partner away.

Fear based behaviours often have the exact opposite effect to what they are intended to achieve.

> *If you love somebody set them free*
> *If you need somebody, call my name*
> *If you want someone, you can do the same*
> *If you want to keep something precious*
> *You got to lock it up and throw away the key*
> *If you want to hold onto your possession*
> *Don't even think about me*
>
> *If you love somebody, set them free*
> STING

The fear of events

The fear of events falls into the fear of the future, the fear of the present and the fear of the past.

These fears can result in endlessly speculating in a person's mind about what is going to happen in the future and in certain cases catastrophising those potential future events, which creates a lack of balance.

Often a person's life experience or past events will have a big effect on their level of fear. If someone has been stung by a wasp they become more fearful of wasps going forward compared to someone who, say, has never been stung by a wasp. Childhood experiences act in this way and create fear based emotions and behaviours in adulthood.

The fear of the present manifests itself in the form of anxiety and depression which can be debilitating and have a negative effect on a person's energy levels.

Salvation lies in the acceptance of events and a person's ability to embrace uncertainty and change whilst having a recognition of the train driver and passenger perspective on life. Fundamentally what is going to happen is going to happen and the fear will serve no purpose other than to spoil the enjoyment of life's journey.

A higher awareness or greater acceptance of the ways things actually are is achieved in part by becoming more aware of the fears and turning them into their mirror images, namely a love or acceptance for whatever the fear was originally of. So a fear of uncertainty becomes a love for uncertainty and so on.

This technique is simply looking at the same thing in a different way. This is what separates a nervous wreck from a spiritual master. They are looking at the same thing, the universe, in a different way. One feels calm and relaxed and the other is in a living hell. Ultimately the choice is yours.

> *A higher awareness or greater acceptance of the ways things actually are is achieved in part by becoming more aware of the fears and turning them into their mirror images, namely a love or acceptance for whatever the fear was originally of.*

10 Mindfulness

The expression that people should learn to 'live in the moment' if they want to find balance, fulfilment and inner peace is quite commonplace.

But what does 'living in the moment' actually mean?

Let us first of all clarify a few terms that are often used with respect to 'living in the moment'. Mindfulness and awareness are both terms that are used to describe the degree to which someone is 'living in the moment'.

According to Buddhist teachings mindfulness has great importance in the context of a person's journey towards enlightenment.

> *Seek to experience the moment more fully as opposed to striving to experience more moments less fully.*

To consider 'the moment' let's take an example of a typical person commuting on their way to work. During the course of the journey the person is thinking about events in the office during the previous week and the sales meeting and salary review that is going to happen in the following week.

Did the person notice the colour of the flowers at the station? Or the different shades of grey clouds in the sky just before entering the office? Or the flirtatious eye contact between the man and woman on the train?

No.

The reality was that 90% of the person's conscious processing power was being used to analyse past and future events and so it can be seen that only 10% was being used for mindfulness or 'living in the present moment'.

For many people the mind has a habit of wandering into the past or the future and therefore cutting down the present moment mindfulness or awareness. The person commuting does the journey everyday and so with the familiarity each time the journey is undertaken the present moment mindfulness tends to reduce each time until a barebones mindfulness state

is reached. It is a bit like taking in events in black and white instead of colour. Only the information that is essential is taken in to leave the mind the processing power to focus on past and future events.

This reduction in mindfulness the more familiar that something becomes explains the law of diminishing returns. This law states that something will be the most exciting the first time you do it and each time after that a little less so until it becomes routine and mundane.

This effect becomes more pronounced the older you get. Think of the ability of a four year old to find everything wondrous and exciting and then think how this amazement seems to wear off as you get older. The four year old's present moment awareness is actually far greater than the adult's.

To visualise mindfulness think of it as a lens through which you view the events or moments in your life. If you were truly 'living in the moment' the lens would be pure and you would absorb and experience every aspect of that moment, the birdsong, the slight breeze, the smell of the lavender and the contrast in shades of green on the holly tree.

In the case of the person commuting, their lens was skewed to view the moment through the past and the future which created a perceived present moment that was not true to the actual present moment. The perceived present moment being a kind of mixture of the past, the present moment and the future.

Mindfulness is a measure of the purity of your lens and your ability to view moments true to how they actually are without prejudices, fears or familiarity filtering taking place.

The present is all there really is in reality. The past and the future are merely constructions of the mind.

Consider for a moment how mindful you are of the present moment. To achieve balance you need to start focussing on the moment and become aware when your mind is wandering or clouding your lens by projecting past fears and prejudices or future speculation into the present moment.

Learn to treat each and every moment with the same sense of wonderment as any previous moment, because it is unique. Try and absorb more of the moment by looking at a picture on the wall, observing the detail, feeling the texture of things, stopping for a moment to listen to the birdsong. You will feel the colour coming back into your life and the spine tingling feeling of being alive.

Balance and fulfilment are the continued expansion of present moment awareness until 100% mindfulness is experienced in every moment.

> *To achieve balance you need to start focussing on the moment and become aware when your mind is wandering or clouding your lens by projecting past fears and prejudices or future speculation into the present moment.*

11 Life gives you what you Need and not what you Want

> *Life will give you whatever experience is most helpful for the evolution of your consciousness. How do you know this is the experience you need? Because this is the experience you are having at the moment.*
>
> ECKHART TOLLE

Life gives you what you need at any given moment to achieve a higher state of consciousness, balance and awareness. The fact that you are reading this book at the moment is a testament to that statement!

But what's going on?

Many people believe that what is happening to them in their life is just a random sequence of events, but they would be wrong to think this.

> *Change the way you look at things and the things you look at will change.*
>
> DR WAYNE DYER

The fact is that a person is connected to everything around them in the same way that the drop is connected to the ocean. If the person moves one way then the universe will move the other way to compensate and balance. In this way the universe always gives a person what they need to reach balance. It is a perfect self correcting system, an automatic teacher that is always contextual to the pupil.

> *Everything in the universe has a purpose. Indeed, the invisible intelligence that flows through everything in a purposeful fashion is also flowing through you.*
>
> DR WAYNE DYER

It is the connection between a person's thoughts which forms the lens through which they view the universe and the mirror image of these which form the universal lens that dictates what moments that person experiences. The interaction and connectivity between the two lenses conspires to give a person what they need to become more balanced in any given moment.

Both lenses come into balance when a person views the universe in the way that it actually is instead of the way that they think it is. This balance is known as the degree of awareness and is ultimately the level of perception that a person has.

> *The physical universe is nothing other than the self curving back within itself to experience itself as spirit, mind and physical matter.*
>
> DEEPAK CHOPRA

The recognition that events happen for a reason has implications regarding the interpretation of coincidences in a person's life. In one sense every event is a coincidence because it is linked to another event. What a person does dictates what the universe does and what the universe does dictates what a person does and so everything becomes a coincidence.

Seems a little weird?

Life gives you what you need and not what you want.

There is one special case that needs to be considered. If a person were to align what they want in life to what they actually need then

what they want = what they need

Because life gives you what you need it would mean in this special case that the person was actually also getting what they want.

So it could be said that balance and fulfilment is a greater understanding of what you actually need as opposed to what you think you need.

When the things that you want are the same as the things that you need you will have reached the point of balance.

Of course we are all unique and the things that we all need will be

different but at the same time many of the things we truly need are the same.

And here is a clue!

> *Love, love, love, love, love, love, love, love, love.*
> *There's nothing you can do that can't be done.*
> *Nothing you can sing that can't be sung.*
> *Nothing you can say but you can learn how to play the game*
> *It's easy.*
> *All you need is love*
> LENNON & MCCARTNEY

12   The Holistic Jigsaw

We have examined one possible view of the world in which our ego, fuelled by fear, convinces us that we are separate to everything around us.

The exact opposite of the ego view is a holistic perspective where we see ourself as an integral part of the whole. In this perspective we see ourselves as a jigsaw piece in the holistic jigsaw. This view creates some interesting philosophical questions.

Consider the whole as being like an engine where we are all different parts but each part is essential to the functioning of the engine. Imagine taking delivery of a new car only to find a spark plug is missing and it doesn't work. No matter how small the bit that is missing it will mean that the whole doesn't work.

Your position in the universe is much the same. Without you it doesn't work!

Although you are a small cog in the universe it cannot function without you. We generally undervalue ourselves because the fact is that the universe will pay any price to you to be part of the universe, subject to one

condition. The condition is that you understand the holistic nature of the universe and align yourself with the rest of the universe. Alignment means that your thoughts and actions are always in your best interest and at the same time are in the best interest of everything around you, known as the win-win scenario.

Another term used to describe the win-win scenario is love. Love for yourself, love for others, love for everything and love for whatever happens.

> *The high destiny of the individual is to*
> *serve rather than to rule.*
> ALBERT EINSTEIN

Alignment with the universe is like a canoeist who can either paddle upstream working against the currents in the river and works hard to paddle a small distance or one who paddles downstream working with the currents and puts in little effort to travel a long distance. You know instinctively in life when you are aligning with the universe, you achieve more by doing less. A bit like hitting the sweetspot on a golf shot – it just feels right.

> *To become master of the universe you must first*
> *learn to be its servant.*

Becoming a master of the universe is a privilege that is dynamically assigned, that is to say it can be given as well as taken away, and is conditional upon adhering to the rules of being a universal servant. If the rules of being a servant to the universe are broken then the privilege of being its master is withdrawn. The universe is like a mirror. If you act in its interests and become its servant then it will become your servant or put another way you will become its master. Of course the opposite is true, if you try to be the universe's master then it will become your master and this is a battle that cannot be won.

> *The degree to which you have become the*
> *universe's servant is another way of saying the*
> *degree to which you have fulfilled your unique*
> *potential.*

Aligning with the universe is acting in a way that is compatible with the way nature works. On the one hand there is competition, survival of the fittest and the sense of working against each other and on the other there is interdependence, symbiosis and a sense of working for each other. These are two seemingly opposite forces that coexist simultaneously in nature.

If you observe the world in which we currently live it is not difficult to see many self-styled masters of the universe, who understand competition and personal gain but who have not woken up to interdependence, sustainability with their environment and the importance of collaboration. Of course their self appointed tenure as a master will be shortlived because they are picking a fight with the universe and will inevitably lose until they learn humility and the rules of the game.

The 'credit crunch' is another term used to describe the process of former masters coming back down to earth.

> *The holistic jigsaw implies that you are a part of me as much as I am a part of you.*

It follows that if I love you and you love me then we are merely recognising our true nature. If you think about it this implies that our true nature is to love each and every person on the planet and if this isn't the case then we are simply in denial!

Balance is achieved by recognising and accepting your true nature. There is individuality and commonality in everyone. The universe cannot function without you and will pay any price for you to fulfill your unique potential. This can only happen when you become a servant to the universe acting in its best interests at all times.

> *Give to receive.*
> *It doesn't work the other way round.*

13 What does Mind, Body and Spirit really mean?

The phrase mind, body and spirit is very well known but not always fully understood. It is a way of expressing the way in which you experience your self in three distinct parts. The expression could have terms for experiencing your self in say five parts or ten parts but it has three. The spirit is the energy that runs through you and links you to all the pieces of the Holistic Jigsaw (universe). It is the divinity that is present in all of us. The spirit is a *collective* term expressing the commonality that runs through all of us. The mind and body are *individual* terms because they are specific to each of us and define us as a unique person. The body is the physical manifestation of the self and the mind is the centre of the self's thoughts.

Balance is achieved by aligning and balancing the mind, body and spirit.

> *The spirit is a **collective** term expressing the commonality that runs through all of us. The mind and body are **individual** terms because they are specific to each of us and define us as a unique person.*

14 The Law of Attraction

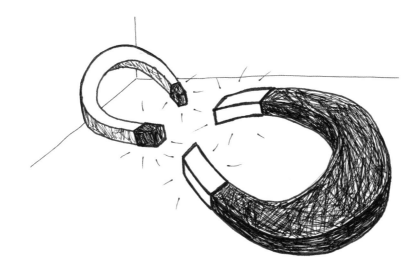

The law of attraction has been written about for centuries and in recent years the book and film *The Secret* has been the most notable on the subject.

In a nutshell, the Law of Attraction states that 'like things attract like things'.

Too simple?

Firstly, let us think about physical things. Everyone is aware of the law of gravity. Basically gravity is the attraction between two masses and it explains why something falls to the ground when dropped, as first observed by Isaac Newton.

Einstein famously told us that Energy and mass are different forms of the same stuff (E=mc2), that we call Energy. So the universe is simply a big ball of energy in different forms with you somewhere in the ball.

So it follows that gravity is simply the attraction that energy fields have for each other. The apple is an energy field, the earth is an energy field and that is why the apple drops from the tree because the energy fields are attracted.

Secondly, think about your thoughts. They control your mental and emotional balance and sense of wellbeing.

Your thoughts are also energy fields transferring information from one place to another. Like any other energy fields the law of attraction applies and so 'like thoughts will attract like thoughts'.

All the energy in the universe is connected, as discussed in the holistic jigsaw, which is why your mobile phone works!

The attraction of thoughts creates an amplifier effect much like a small signal from a guitar becoming a large sound from the speakers at a concert.

> *Your thoughts and your feelings create your Life.*
> *Physical reality is a reflection of your inner subjective*
> *reality.*
>
> THE SECRET

It is as though the physical reality of your life is actually determined by your thoughts in the first instance, which is then amplified by the law of attraction.

> *The external world is only a manifestation of the*
> *activities of the mind itself, and …the mind grasps*
> *it as an external world simply because of its habit of*
> *discrimination and false reasoning.*
>
> BUDDHA

One of the bestselling books of all time, *Think and Grow Rich* (1937), discusses the importance of controlling your thoughts to achieve success and goes on to explain the energy that thoughts have and their ability to attract other thoughts.

'Your wish is my command'

You can have whatever you want on one condition. You tell me what you want!

THE UNIVERSE

The universe is acting in the same way as Aladdin's lamp. It says 'tell me what you want in the form of your thoughts' and 'Your wish is my command' and it will manifest the thoughts into a physical reality.

So why am I not getting what I want?

'I can't get no satisfaction' as the Rolling Stones famously sang.

Put simply, to get more of what you want in your life you have to be more disciplined in the way you think and think more about the things you want. This is a positive thought process or positivity.

Many people think about the things they don't want in their life and this has the effect of attracting more of the same. This is a negative thought process or negativity.

> *Remember to align your thoughts on what you want with what you need as these are unique to you.*

In a person's thought process there are the conscious and the subconscious thoughts which both deliver the wish list to the universe.

To achieve balance it is therefore important to think about what you want both consciously and subconsciously and ensure there are no negative embedded thoughts in your subconscious.

> *In a person's thought process there are the conscious and the subconscious thoughts which both deliver the wish list to the universe.*

15 The House of Smoke and Mirrors

Most people would say that the events in their life are unconnected to them and out of their control. This perception is known as an outside in perspective, that is to say, that the perception is that life comes at them from the outside.

It is fairly normal for people to blame others for things that do not work out in their life and the things that go wrong often take the form of repetitive behavioural patterns. For example, often a failed relationship is followed by another failed relationship with similar reasons for the breakdown.

So the important question is, 'Who is always at the scene of the crime? Whose actions are creating the same results?'

The answer, of course, is that each and every one of us is the centre of our own life and the reason for what is happening in their life.

It would therefore seem a good idea to consider the inside out approach to perceiving our lives to examine what it is that we are doing that is creating our reality.

In this perception it is a person's thoughts and behaviour that are

shaping their reality.

Imagine you are the centre of your universe and everything that you perceive around you is dependent on how you perceived those things.

> *This is the house of smoke and mirrors and in this perception* what *you experience from the universe depends on* how *you are experiencing it.*

You are the central character in your own universe and the way everyone behaves is dependent on the lens through which you are viewing events.

What you notice is what you are looking for. Have you ever bought a red car and then you start to notice red cars on the road? They were always there but you just hadn't noticed them.

If you haven't looked at the world in this way before then this may seem a little strange. If you think for a moment about the Law of Attraction which says essentially that what you think about is what is attracted to you then this concurs with the house of smoke and mirrors concept. Your reality is determined from within.

This creates exciting possibilities because it enables you to gain some control over your life. What you may previously have thought was unpredictable is in fact predictable. The whole process is governed by your thoughts and to connect with what you want you simply need to be more disciplined with your mind and your thoughts.

I think we need to start thinking about the universe in a slightly different way. Firstly everything that at first glance would appear to be a certainty is not necessarily so. The way we perceive things can play tricks on us and we need to be aware of that.

There is a saying, 'Improbable but not impossible', and this means that assumptions should never be made that anything is impossible. Part of the journey through this book is to open our mind to possibilities that we perhaps hadn't thought of or hadn't thought to be possible. If our minds are closed then it is not possible to take this journey.

> *The limit of what is possible is the limit of what someone thinks is possible. To make something possible then you need to truly believe it is possible.*

16 The Field of All and No Possibilities

Have you ever had a radio aerial or a TV aerial and tried to move it around to get a better signal? You will find that at a certain angle the signal is the weakest but if you move the aerial so that it is at 90 degrees to that position then the signal will be at its strongest.

Let us use this analogy to describe the way you are experiencing the universe. Imagine yourself to be an aerial operating in a large field of energy which is basically what you and the universe are.

You can change the angle of reception of your aerial which is another way of saying that you are changing the way you are looking at the universe. You are changing your perception.

If we consider the extremes you would find that if you looked at the universe in a certain way you would experience the weakest signal. At this point you would experience the field of no possibilities. To visualise this, imagine going to a railway station and finding that it was not possible to catch a train to go anywhere. You know the places you want to go exist but it is just not possible to get there.

You are out of tune with the universe in a mental state of disharmony and as a consequence nothing would seem to be possible.

This way of looking at things is commonly referred to as depression. When someone becomes depressed their field of possibilities becomes less and less and this results in a feeling of helplessness and that nothing is possible.

If you were to change the angle of reception of your aerial, or your perspective, to a position that is at 90 degrees to the zero reception line then you would tune into the field of all possibilities.

This way of looking at things is known as being manic. When someone is manic there is a huge feeling of energy and euphoria.

You are in tune with the universe in a mental state of harmony and as a result anything seems possible.

Again let us visualise going to a station and at this point you could find a train to any possible destination. Quite literally this is the point at which anything is possible and this is known as the field of all possibilities.

The field of no possibilities and the field of all possibilities are the extremes and of course most people are somewhere in the middle. It could be said that someone is a pessimist or an optimist and this would indicate which way their aerial tends to point.

But the important thing is that your aerial can be moved or, put another way, your perception can be changed to a more balanced position.

And of course this is what this book is all about, hopefully helping you understand what factors affect balance and how to fine tune them.

So what affects your perception?

There are, of course, several things that affect perception but two of the main things are your brain chemistry and the way you think which is known as your cognitive process. The cognitive process is a bit like the software your brain is running. These factors dictate the lens through which you view the universe.

> *The field of no possibilities and the field of all possibilities are the extremes and, of course, most people are somewhere in the middle.*
>
> *But the important thing is that your aerial can be moved or, put another way, your perception can be changed to a more balanced position.*

17 Brain Chemistry

If you imagine for a moment your perception to be like wearing a pair of glasses. Some people would be wearing dark glasses which might be the equivalent to a depressed view and others would be wearing multicoloured glasses which would be a sunny view of life. Somewhere in the middle would be a colourless set of glasses which would be a reality pair, that it to say through which things can be seen as they actually are in a balanced way.

> *The two main factors that determine the glasses you are wearing, or your perception, are your brain chemistry and your cognitive process.*

The brain's function is to sense information on up to 5 channels, sight, smell, taste, sound and touch, and to translate this into a mental picture that can then be used to decide what actions if any need to be taken. For example the mental picture might be 'your hand is in a fire' and the action selected could be 'remove hand from the fire quickly'. These computations are happening every second of a person's life and often without someone being aware of it.

The brain sends information via neurotransmitters using neuro-chemicals such as dopamine and serotonin. The brain is complex and so every person has slightly different genetic brain chemistry and this creates a slightly different perception for each of us, in a similar way that a fingerprint is unique.

> *A common assumption is that other people perceive things in the same way that you do. This is not the case.*

As well as the genetic brain chemistry there is also the effect on a person's brain chemistry caused by the food you eat, the caffeine, the alcohol, and the drugs you take and so on.

Caffeine has the effect of increasing a person's serotonin levels so that they feel stimulated and more awake whilst alcohol temporarily increases serotonin levels and then depletes the serotonin in the longer term causing a depressed perspective. Alcohol also causes the body to release stress hormones such as cortisol which have the affect of increasing stress levels.

Sound, often in the form of music, will affect a person's brain chemistry and perspective. Heavy Rock can lift the mood and classical music can bring the mood down or vice versa depending on your preference!

Light will also affect a person's serotonin levels and consequent mood level and perception. As SAD (Seasonal Affective Disorder) sufferers will testify, low light levels in the winter cause a low mood level and a feeling of depression.

Physical exercise is known to have a positive effect on neurotransmitters, to release endorphins and to create new neurons (nerve cells) in a process known as neuro-genesis.

> *In a nutshell, anything that can be experienced through a person's senses will affect their brain chemistry and therefore that person's mood level and perception.*

One of the biggest regulators of brain chemistry is actually a person's sleep pattern. More sleep tends to bring the mood down and less sleep tends to bring the mood level up.

In a nutshell, anything that can be experienced through a person's senses will affect their brain chemistry and therefore that person's mood level and perception.

It can be seen that a person's lifestyle choices will affect their brain chemistry which, in turn, affects their mood level, perception and balance. It is therefore important to ensure that good habits, known as positive behaviours, are put in place to achieve balance.

In many instances, drugs such as antidepressants are prescribed to mask the effect of the poor lifestyle choices that a person makes.

It is often the case that a person will naturally do exactly the wrong thing to counteract their mood and create balance.

For example if a person is depressed they may seek comfort in alcohol which is a depressant and so that creates a vicious circle.

More alcohol = lower mood = more alcohol and so on.

The same is true for people with a high mood level who often reach for caffeine or cocaine or any stimulants they can find.

More stimulants = higher mood = more stimulants and so on.

In many instances, drugs such as antidepressants are prescribed to mask the effect of the poor lifestyle choices that a person makes.

It is often the case that a person will naturally do exactly the wrong thing to counteract their mood and create balance.

These are known as destructive behaviours.

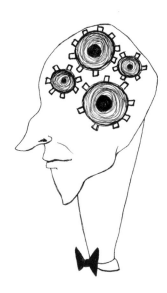

18 The Cognitive Process

If you think of your brain as a type of computer then the cognitive process would be like the software or computer program that it was running.

So where does the cognitive process come from?

Of course this is the subject of the 'nature or nurture' debate but it would be fair to say that the cognitive process is likely to be a mixture of a person's genetic mental process and their learnt mental process.

As soon as someone is born they learn that when they cry food appears and then in time they listen to sounds and become aware of language. This adds to their cognitive process capability and as the child becomes older they continue to learn based on 'cause and effect'.

'Cause and effect' is when something is tried and the reaction is observed.

Over the course of their lifetime, different people will end up with different cognitive processes because, firstly, everyone has a unique genetic make up and, secondly, the situations they have encountered in their lives will also be different.

It is often the case that if someone has experienced a painful event in their life, like, for example, being stung by a wasp, then they will have a disproportionate fear of wasps. Somebody else who has never been stung by a wasp is likely to underestimate the risk posed by wasps, or have too little fear.

The ideal position to achieve balance would be to have the fear equivalent to the actual risk posed by wasps in a person's cognitive process. Too much fear of something is as bad as too little.

Often imbalances in the cognitive process can be formed in the childhood years and this can lead to low 'self esteem' or 'self love' which can act as drivers to destructive behaviours in adulthood such as alcohol and drug addictions.

If you imagine your cognitive process as being like a ball of wool that is formed over the years then inevitably knots will form. To achieve balance it is important to identify where the knots are and talk about them openly to relieve the pressure. It is common for the knots to be left because someone might not want to talk about them. This generally leads to anger, frustration, depression and destructive behaviour patterns.

A person has to make choices every second of the day as to what is the best action to take given the circumstances that they encounter. The choice of action can become a reflex reaction, or learnt behaviour, and consequently doesn't feel like a choice. For example the reflex reaction might be that if someone offers you advice that you take it as criticism and react angrily. In Cognitive Behaviour Therapy or CBT a person's balance is improved by analysing the reflex destructive behaviours in their cognitive process and replacing them with cognitive choices that are more balanced and are the best action at that moment. In the previous example, if someone offers you advice it would be a healthier response to thank them for the feedback and take note of the comments.

Famously in his book, *Man's search for meaning*, Vicktor Frankl demonstrated that when everything else is outside your control, as was the case in the concentration camp he found himself in, that the only thing that can be controlled is the choice you have over how you react to something.

How you react to something is always your choice, no matter what happens.

It can be seen that choosing the right action at the right time is the key to balance and to do this your cognitive process needs to be balanced.

19 Beliefs, Values and Behaviour

People are faced with the choice of what is the best action to take every second of the day. Right action is the best action to take at any given moment and is always the win-win choice, the best action for the individual and the collective.

Out of all the possible choices of action at any given moment there is only one Right Action.

Just as some people are better at golf than others and get better scores, it follows that some people are better than others at selecting the Right Action at any given moment.

One person might choose the Right Action say 3/10 whilst another person might choose the Right Action 9/10.

This will have a large impact on how balanced a person feels.

So why are some people better than others at choosing the Right Action?

The starting point is the Right View. This is a person's view on life, their perspective, and it acts like a person's map or compass. It follows that if their map is not very good then it is unlikely that they will make good choices. If you imagine driving a car with a poor map it's clear that you will make poor choices as to the best direction compared to if you had an accurate, comprehensive map. A person's View or map is learnt over many years through often painful life experiences, but the life lessons are fundamentally the same for all of us and have been throughout history.

People are simply reinventing the wheel in their lives, the only thing that is unique is how they do it and at what speed.

How accurate a person's map is, compared to the way things actually are, is known as a person's awareness.

In the middle of a person's view or beliefs and their choice of action are their intentions or values.

Values such as honesty, integrity, fairness, trust will lead to the choice of Right Action whereas values such as dishonesty, unfairness, and untrustworthiness will lead to the choice of wrong action.

A person's values are said to be either sustainable in the case of positive values or unsustainable in the case of negative values.

Clearly a person's degree of balance is conditional on their view of life, their values and their ability to choose the right action. High Awareness people learn to select right action intuitively, often without any conscious thought.

> *Failure is not a single, cataclysmic event. You don't fail overnight. Instead, failure is a few errors in judgement, repeated every day.* JIM ROHN

A bundle or sequence of actions is known as a behaviour or, if it is often repeated, then it becomes a learnt behaviour or habit. Like anything, some habits are positive or right behaviour for balance while some are negative.

It is often the case that a person instinctively selects the wrong learnt behaviour for a given situation, in much the same way as they select the wrong remedy such as alcohol or drugs.

A depressed person may sleep and do no exercise which would be the wrong behaviour and someone on a high would not sleep and go partying which would also be the wrong behaviour.

It is true that the same behaviour will always lead to the same result.

There is a well known analogy of a bluebottle fly that repeatedly bangs its head on a window. Someone says to the fly that if it just moves up slightly then it can fly out of the window and be free. The fly just carries on with its learnt behaviour and keeps banging its head.

Have you ever given advice to someone who doesn't listen in this way?

The same action leads to the same result.

Intelligence is a measure of a person's awareness of and ability to adapt to this reality.

20 | Are you a Giver or a Taker?

> *My father said there were two kinds of people in the world: givers and takers. The takers may eat better, but the givers sleep better.*
>
> MARLO THOMAS

It is the old wisdom that says that fundamentally there are two types of people in this world, givers and takers.

The crucial question, though, is which one are you?

Let us first of all investigate what giving and taking actually means. As we have already seen the right action is one where you create a win-win scenario between you as an individual and everything else which is called the collective.

If you are a giver it means that over a period of time you are creating a bigger win for everything around you than you are for yourself. You are selfless.

So what is wrong with this approach?

The problem is that this lifestyle is not sustainable and as a result it can only be maintained for a certain period of time.

If you imagine your life as being like a rechargeable battery then the charge of a giver will tend to run down until they are no longer able to give any more.

For this reason you will find that most people who suffer nervous breakdowns tend to be givers by nature.

They quite literally want to help others and forget to help themselves.

> *Successful people are always looking for opportunities to help others. Unsuccessful people are always asking, 'What's in it for me?'*
>
> BRIAN TRACY

If you are a taker it means that over a period of time you are trying to create a bigger win for yourself than for everything around you. You are selfish. This tactic often works in the short-term but when people become aware of your true colours this strategy does not work well in the long term.

The internet has meant that selfish short-term strategies to, say, defraud people or provide a poor service cannot last for long because everyone gets to know about it. The long-term damage to a person's reputation is always greater than the short-term gain.

Achieving balance is about balancing the give and take. People tend to be naturally one way or the other and so it is necessary to learn new habits, like a right-footed footballer learning to kick with his left foot. A sustainable lifestyle is always more productive in the long term than an unbalanced lifestyle which can only last in the short-term.

> *Only those who have learned the power of sincere and selfless contribution experience life's deepest joy: true fulfilment.*
>
> ANTHONY ROBBINS

21 | Karma

> *What goes around..................comes around.*
>
> JUSTIN TIMBERLAKE

Most people are familiar with the concept of Karma. Philosophers and physicists have talked about it for centuries. In physics there are the terms 'action' and 'reaction' which form part of Isaac Newton's third law of motion.

To philosophers there are the terms 'cause' and 'effect' and 'You reap what you sow' and to musicians, 'What goes around comes around'.

So it is true to say that lots of different people are describing the same thing in different ways.

Karma implies a connection between you and everything else in the universe.

So what does Karma really mean?

> *Every action creates an energy that returns to us in like kind. This is true of both positive and negative actions.*
>
> DEEPAK CHOPRA

In other words whatever you do or think will have an effect on the energy field that you are part of, which in our case is the universe. What is more, the energy field will always seek to counterbalance what it is you are doing or thinking. Like a guitar string, if you pluck it one way then it vibrates the other way.

> *The universe has a perfect accounting system and no debt goes unpaid. People essentially reap what they sow.*
>
> DEEPAK CHOPRA

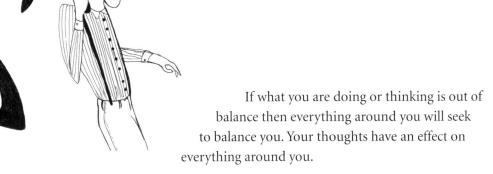

If what you are doing or thinking is out of balance then everything around you will seek to balance you. Your thoughts have an effect on everything around you.

Sounds a bit weird?

Previously we have established that:

> **Physical reality is a reflection of your inner subjective reality.**
>
> THE SECRET

So it is as though what you experience is a reflection or mirror image of what you think. The only time that this is balanced is when your thoughts are true to your self, which means the reflection or your self image is the same as who you are. This is known as self love. This is how balance is achieved. Balance is simply a measure of the degree to which who you are and who you think you are, your self-image, are aligned.

> *Balance is simply a measure of the degree to which who you are and who you think you are, your self-image, are aligned.*

So how do I make karma work for me?

The universe acts as a kind of dynamic energy exchange in which what goes out must come in, what goes up must come down. So basically you need to give whatever it is you want.

> *If you want money then give money*
>
> *If you want love then give love*
>
> *Just give whatever it is you want*
>
> *Give to receive. Where have we heard this before?*

22 The Inflatable Lifestyle – the House of Cards

Just like the three pigs who built their houses out of straw and bricks, people build their lives on different foundations.

> *Treasure your relationships, not your possessions.*
> ANTHONY J. D'ANGELO

A common scenario in the modern world is to chase material possessions and empires at the expense of focusing on relationships.

How many times do you hear, 'I have been so busy and not able to call'? This may go on from one year until the next.

The question is, 'So busy doing what?' What is so important that someone does not keep in touch with their friends? What could be more important?

It is as though we are all running around like headless chickens trying to convince ourselves that we are so busy, when fundamentally we are not.

> *We are just busy doing the wrong things, the things that have little value.*

How many people buy expensive clothes not because of the quality but basically to say to everyone else that they can afford a more expensive shirt than other people? This 'one upmanship' is accepted as normal behaviour.

Then there are people who perceive themselves to be powerful based on their wealth or job title. This is very temporary ego-based power. When the job or the money goes then so does the power.

The 'friends' and associates of the power people are like bees around a honeypot until the power goes and then they disappear quickly when there is no advantage to be gained. They are temporary and are only there for self gain. Do you know anyone like that?

> *If you are going to build something in the air it is always better to build castles than houses of cards.*
> GEORG C. LICHTENBERG

In short, inflatable lifestyles based on temporary transient factors are very unstable and tend to go over very quickly, like a pack of cards, when a few things go wrong.

Balance is about choosing to live your life on sound foundations and not becoming intoxicated with a short-lived ego-based lifestyle.

> *You never have to impress real friends because*
> *they like you just as you are.*

To build a sustainable and stable life people must think about relationships above possessions, values above fashions, adaptation above being 'stuck in your ways' and collaboration above self interest.

Don't fall into the trap of being the proverbial 'fool on the hill', aloof and unconnected to everyone else.

Just be authentic and real and seek to connect with people rather than set yourself apart from them. This is your true nature.

> *Real power comes from being true to who you are,*
> *not from trying to impress everyone with who you*
> *would like to be.*

23 Time – the most precious Commodity

There is an interesting phenomenon that occurs when you zoom in and out of ego states. In Steve Taylor's book *Making Time,* he observes that time appears to happen at different speeds depending on your ego state. If you are fully absorbed in something in an ego state e.g. playing the PlayStation then time appears to run fast and if you are in a non ego state e.g meditation then time appears to run slow.

So depending on how you perceive yourself you can affect the amount of time you live for! Or at least how long it appears to you that you live for.

> *Time is free, but it's priceless. You can't own it, but you can use it. You can't keep it, but you can spend it. Once you've lost it you can never get it back.*
>
> HARVEY MACKAY

Einstein told us that time was a relative concept, meaning that the experience of time is dependent on the relationship between the observer and what is being observed.

> *This means that if you are able to vary and control the way you are observing your life, which is your perspective, then you can experience time in different ways.*

If you were able to push this to its extremes then you would find that you were able to experience time standing still on the one hand and time running superfast where all events could be experienced simultaneously on the other.

This is what spiritual masters call the Nirvana condition or enlightenment.

To experience time in the full range of possible ways requires discipline and control.

So what about our everyday lives?

Many people attach a lot of importance to material possessions and the pursuit of money.

If you think about it, the commodity that is finite, in scarce supply, is the amount of time in someone's life. Moreover, nobody knows whether the available time in their life will come to an end the following day, the following year or in a number of years.

> *I believe every human has a finite number of heartbeats. I don't intend to waste any of mine.*
>
> NEIL ARMSTRONG

In this context it can be seen that it is time that is the most valuable commodity a person can have, not money. If you left this earth tomorrow what use would your possessions be?

How many people do you know that have had a near-death experience or a terminal illness and have said that the way they view their life has completely changed. Why wait for such an incident in your life to change the way you view your time?

If people looked at life in this perspective it would inevitably change the way that they used their time, with a likelihood that, due to its scarcity, it would be used a lot more meaningfully. Time is too precious to waste.

The question to ask is would you have changed anything in the preceding 5 years in the way you have used your time if it was your funeral today? If the answer is 'yes', then it is time to consider making lifestyle changes now. As the old phrase says, 'Nobody puts on their headstone that they wish they had spent more time at work.'

> *In your life, time is the most precious commodity because of its limited supply and consequent unlimited value. Balance is achieved by valuing your time closer to its real value and using it to focus on what really matters.*

If you think of antiques dealers or auctioneers, then a large part of their job is placing valuations on the items they are looking to sell or buy. Their success or failure is to a large part determined by the accuracy of those valuations.

Your ability to achieve balance is also governed by the valuations you place on the different aspects that constitute your life. In much the same way as the auctioneer, if you are attaching great value to things that are of little value and too little value to things of great value then you will not achieve balance.

The valuations you are making are taking place every second of every day, often in a subconscious pre-programmed way without your knowledge.

> *Not everything that can be counted counts, and not everything that counts can be counted.*
>
> ALBERT EINSTEIN

Let us first consider you as being on a beach building a sandcastle that represents your life. There are a number of people on the beach and everyone builds a different sandcastle. One person builds a simple lump of sand and someone else builds several turrets and flags and a drawbridge and so on. Everyone is different and what they achieve in their life is different, as represented by their sandcastle.

Then the tide comes in and what happens? All the sandcastles are flattened and no matter how grand they were the result is the same for everyone. Nothing can stand in the way of the sea. This analogy could represent your time on this earth and the inevitability of it coming to an end.

If you look at things in this way then it can be seen that material possessions, job titles at work, fashion and so on are very temporary and transient, like a small wavelet on the sea, and as such are of a lower value in the grand scheme of things.

The idea of permanence is exchanged for the idea that your life is really only ever for rent, in the sense that you never fully own or control it.

Many people base their foundations in life on the ownership of possessions such as property, assets and belongings and this is flawed as the sea will always come in and take them away. The valuations on them are too high, as they don't offer security, any more than sandcastles do.

On the other hand what valuation do you place on yourself?

> *I've always thought*
> *that I would love to live by the sea*
> *to travel the world alone*
> *and live more simply*
> *I have no idea what's happened to that dream*
> *Cos there's really nothing left here to stop me*
> *It's just a thought, only a thought*
> *But if my life is for rent and I don't learn to buy*
> *Well I deserve nothing more than I get*
> *Cos nothing I have is truly mine*
>
> LIFE FOR RENT   DIDO

Many caring people find it hard to value themselves in a way that is true to who they really are.

> *The limit of self love is by definition the limit of the love that can be shown to others.*

In many cases and for many different reasons people tend to undervalue themselves, which has the effect of them undervaluing the people around them. This has a significant impact on their ability to find balance.

> *Too many people overvalue what they are not and undervalue what they are.*
> MALCOLM FORBES

And what is the valuation on your actions?

As much as possessions are temporary, the impact of your actions are in some ways permanent. Consider the time spent with children, with other relationships, teaching others or setting up or working with a charity. Your actions have a direct impact on others and in turn may influence how others interact with others and so on. There is a cascading effect which flows outwards and never ends, a chain reaction of sorts.

It is therefore your actions and interactions with others that are eternal and should be given the highest valuation. When you are gone people will not remember what car you had, but they will respect the actions of your children, friends and associates and the impact you had on those people.

> *The greatness of a man is not in how much wealth he acquires, but in his integrity and his ability to affect those around him positively.*
> BOB MARLEY

To achieve balance, consciously ask yourself what valuations you are placing on different aspects of your life and on others around you and make adjustments where they are needed.

All people are equal but, at the same time, they are all unique and should be valued as such. If you are looking up to people or down at people you need to make some adjustments on your valuations. Respect for everyone is the only sustainable path.

> *There is no such thing as bad people, only good people doing bad things.*

25 Fulfilling your Potential

There is one thing each of us is better at than anyone else on the planet...........and that is being ourselves.

Everyone has a unique potential in this world and the purpose of your life is to firstly realise what that potential is and secondly to fulfill that potential.

Your potential can be split into two main areas.

On the one hand, your unique potential could be defined as your ability in given tasks e.g. How fast can you run? What is your IQ? How good are you at woodwork? Can you sing?

Your ability at different things could be gauged relative to others by comparison.

On the other hand, fulfilling your potential could be measured by saying it is the degree to which you have found balance and inner peace. This potential is the same for all of us.

> *A person is a success if they get up in the morning and go to bed at night and in between do what they want to do.*
> BOB DYLAN

The limit of what can be achieved is determined by two factors. Firstly your unique potential at, say, running, and secondly your motivation, application and dedication to running. This could be called your positive mental attitude or positivity.

The only things stopping you reaching your potential are the limitations you put on yourself.

So the maximum possible achievement, i.e. to fulfill your potential, would occur when you combine your unique ability with 100% positivity.

It should be noted that someone may have less potential than you but achieve more if their positivity is higher than yours.

So it can be seen that fulfilling your potential has everything to do with your positivity or mental attitude. To fulfill your overall potential you need to have 100% positivity at all times. This means that you always give your best and ensure you are physically and mentally at your peak performance.

> *A common mistake is to underestimate your potential and not give your best at every moment. This inevitably leads to not fulfilling your true potential.*

Often people who are blessed with the greatest ability and potential are also cursed with the demons that go with genius e.g. George Best, Kurt Cobain and Frank Bruno

Fulfilling your potential can be a tough road and the higher you aim the tougher it becomes.

> *The potential of the average person is like a huge ocean unsailed, a new continent unexplored, a world of possibilities waiting to be released and channelled toward some great good.*
>
> BRIAN TRACY

Achieving balance and inner peace runs hand in hand with fulfilling your potential. Listen to your inner self, and not always to others to work out what your potential is.

> *Fulfilling your potential runs hand in hand with a positive attitude and a desire to push the frontiers of your mind to truly find out where the limits are. The limits are not who you are but a fear of who you are not.*

26 The Natural Frequency and Flow of Life

If you tapped a tuning fork you would find that it vibrates at a certain frequency specific to that tuning fork, known as the resonant frequency. The natural frequency would depend on the characteristics of the tuning fork.

If you imagine all of us to be like unique tuning forks it can be seen that each of us has our own natural frequency. Becoming aware of your frequency is the first stage to actually living in harmony with it.

So what does the natural frequency mean?

The first component of your natural frequency is timing. Any comedian will tell you that it is often the timing more than the content that will make people laugh.

Put simply, *when* you do things is just as important as *what* you are doing.

Forcing the pace and trying to move too fast is a common mistake people make and is often caused by a lack of awareness and sensitivity to what is happening around that person.

> **Life behaves in exactly the opposite way to what you would expect. Forcing the pace slows you down whilst going with the flow speeds you up. The choice on timing is always yours.**

In any given moment we have already seen that there is only one best action that forms the 'win-win' between the individual and the collective.

In terms of what you do, the range of how you react to a given situation is determined by the range of possible actions and reactions in your 'toolbox' and your choice of which one to apply.

Some people always react in the same way to certain situations. This could mean that they have a limited number of possible reactions available to them and tend to follow conditioned responses in autopilot mode.

Alternatively, someone may simply always choose the same way to react

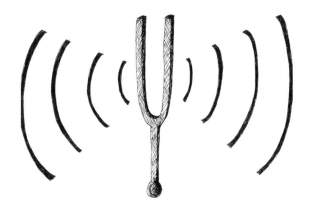

despite having the ability to react in lots of different ways.

Either way, what you do or how relevant and appropriate it is to your environment determines how close you are to your natural frequency.

> *Flowing with the natural frequency of life means choosing the right action at the right time.*

> *Tuning into and applying your unique natural frequency is the key to achieving balance.*

So how can I live in tune with my natural frequency?

The first step is to acknowledge and become aware that the natural frequency exists.

The second step is to listen carefully to the feedback that is happening all around you. Learn to become the owl that looks and listens, sits in the tree and observes and becomes more aware of its environment.

> *Achieving Balance involves adapting and connecting your own actions with the ever-changing environment in which you find yourself.*

Physicists talk about causality, which is the relationship between cause and the effect. In essence, you need to become more aware of the relationship between what you are doing and the effect it is having on everything around you.

The third step is to work on increasing the possible number of actions and reactions that you have in your 'toolbox' so that you have a better chance of choosing an action that is the most appropriate for any given situation.

The fourth step is to introduce more adaptability, flexibility and context into your actions and reactions so that you do not always behave in the same way and what you do is more in tune with and more appropriate to the situation you are in. Always make your choices consciously and become more aware of conditioned, reflex responses.

Finally, you need to become more conscious of the timing and fine-tune it. If you are more aware of the natural flow of things you can achieve more with less effort. The harder you push the more resistance there is. You will find an optimum pace which is the balance between pushing and not pushing. When you are at the natural frequency you will know it instinctively, it just feels right.

In life you will always meet obstacles. Everyone has tried to smash these down by 'banging your head against a brick wall'. The natural frequency is all about being aware of the obstacles but flowing around them like a river along the path of least resistance, the path of least effort. Work smarter, not harder.

> *Your life should flow, at your natural frequency,*
> *along the path of least resistance, like a river,*
> *going around the obstacles towards your*
> *destination to fulfill your destiny.*

Another aspect of the natural flow is whether you are 'chasing' life or 'attracting' it.

It is the old adage that if you are chasing after a partner then you cannot find one. It is as though you have a sign on your forehead saying you are desperate. On the other hand when you have a partner you suddenly receive loads of offers from prospective partners.

Forcing the pace, or chasing life, has the effect of reducing the number of options open to you whereas tuning in to your natural frequency, or attracting life, has the effect of increasing the number of options available to you. In a nutshell, you become a stronger and stronger magnet the more in tune you are with your natural frequency.

> *If you become perfectly in tune with your natural*
> *frequency you become a magnet of infinite power*
> *and all options become available to you, the field*
> *of all possibilities.*

27 What is Reality? The Observer and the Observed

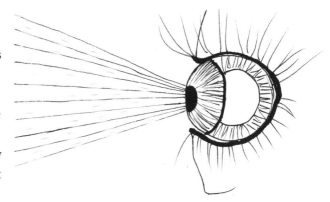

What is reality? This is clearly a big subject and many tomes have been written about it. To achieve balance it is important to have a big-picture overview of what reality is, or at least what people think it is.

> *As far as the laws of mathematics refer to reality, they are not certain, and as far as they are certain, they do not refer to reality.*
>
> ALBERT EINSTEIN

Firstly, reality exists as a result of the relativity between two poles. The poles are an observer and something that is being observed. A good analogy would be to think of the two poles as a camera (the observer) and the subject of the picture (the observed).

There is a layer that sits in between the observer and the observed which is known as the process of observation.

Deepak Chopra says that, "Reality is really the unknown and unmanifest becoming the known and the manifest at the intersection of the observer and the observed. Law is the process or set of rules that facilitate and govern this process. During this process the observer becomes the observed and vice versa."

The three components of reality are mind, spirit and body, which are essentially the same thing as the observer, the process of observation and the observed.

Think for a moment about the difference between a single-frame camera and a video camera. Your reality is like a series of single frames being experienced in a video sequence.

The relative motion between the observer and the observed determines the speed or frame rate of your reality and as such determines the perception of time. If the frame rate is slow then time appears to run slow and if the frame rate is fast it appears to run fast. The extremes are when time stands still and the frame rate is zero or when everything is experienced simultaneously when the frame rate is infinite. These equate to the field of no possibilities and the field of all possibilities.

The observer and the observed are connected with each other. This means that what you observe is directly linked to how you are observing it.

> *All of us are watchers – of television, of time clocks, of traffic on the freeway – but few are observers. Everyone is looking, not many are seeing.*
>
> PETER M. LESCHAK

Reality can be any permutation between something or nothing, between energy or matter (non energy) or between a one and a zero. Fundamentally these are all just different words to express the same thing.

The observer can view the observed from an infinite number of perspectives. Likewise a fixed observer could view an infinite number of different permutations of the observed.

It follows that there are an infinite number of single frame observer/ observed permutations and therefore an infinite number of sequences of observer/ observed permutations. In a nutshell, the starting point for the universe is that anything is possible, so it would be a good idea if we all started with this idea.

So what does this mean!?

Firstly, your life is a sequence of observer / observed permutations. This is what consciousness is.

To some it would appear that their life is out of their control. Whereas the fact is that a person's reality can be co-created because observer and observed are linked.

It could be said that there are an infinite number of ways of experiencing your 'self' and your life is simply one of those permutations.

Your reality is specific to you. Everyone has a different reality. When you encounter other people it is at the intersection of your respective universes and realities.

The universe is in perfect balance. If you are not experiencing this balance it is because the way you are observing it is out of balance. Finding balance and inner peace is about 'tuning in' to what already is. This is why it doesn't have to be hard work. Think of it as tuning in to a radio frequency that you didn't know existed. Stone Age people didn't have mobile phones, not because the frequency wasn't there but because they didn't know it was there. Awareness is the degree to which someone has discovered the 'higher' frequencies.

> ***The primary constituent elements of your universe are your thoughts.***

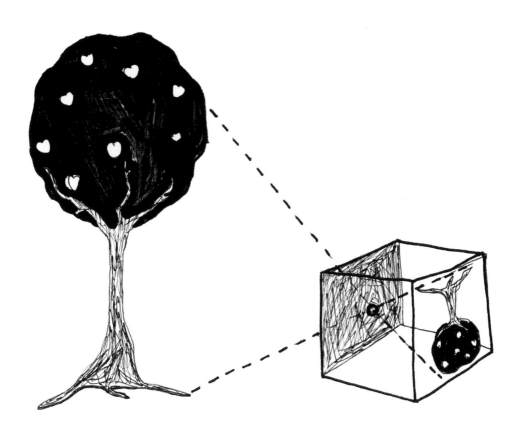

The universe acts as an inverted mirror in much the same way as a pinhole camera.

The balance point between the observer and the observed is found at the pinhole where the observer and observed become the same thing. This is the Nirvana point sought by spiritual masters.

At the pinhole the observer, the process of observation and the observed converge to become the same thing.

At this point the information stored, which holds an infinite amount of data about the tree and its surround, is compressed to a very small, almost zero size. This is the point where the infinite is converging on becoming nothing, another example of the co-existence of opposites. Try to imagine this convergence point as being at the centre of a sphere. This is the point from which any observer/observed permutation can be accessed and is in effect the field of all possibilities, the point of unity and oneness. *This point is accessible to all of us.*

> *What we create and observe is a subset or small part of what the universe is capable of. Balance is the convergence and alignment with the infinite mind, energy and possibilities of the universe. Achieving balance is a possibility for everyone.*

If you are observing out of balance with the observed then what you experience will seek to balance you and will be amplified. You essentially experience your own bias magnified several times.

> *Every day the existence of the universe depends on whether you care enough to create it.*
>
> PAUL WILLIAMS

28 Are we Real or Virtual Reality?

Reality is merely an illusion, albeit a very persistent one.

ALBERT EINSTEIN

Emptiness is a concept associated with Buddhist philosophy and a well known paradox is

Form is emptiness and emptiness is form.

So what is going on? How can reality be an illusion when it feels so real?

Most people would say that their life is 'real' and would think of the universe as being like a big set of solid snooker balls orbiting around and bashing into each other, solid and 3D.

To experience reality we need to perceive it. In any given moment, our brains take the readings from our senses and convert them into a single picture. It could be a pattern of 1s and 0s like a digital photo. This is the 'perception of' reality, it is not solid balls flying around but simply a subtle pattern of 1s and 0s that can be decoded to represent an infinity of different 'real' permutations.

As we have discussed reality is the relativity between an observer and the observed. There is a special point when the two poles become the same thing exactly in balance. This could also be said to be the convergence point of the 'perception of' your life and the 'real' life.

The question is, are we experiencing the 'perception of' our lives as opposed to the 'real' life.

There is a special point of balance where the 'perception of' your life would appear to be exactly the same as your 'real' life and you would not be able to tell the difference.

Let's do a thought experiment to explain further. You are playing a flight simulator on the PlayStation. It is quite realistic but you are aware that you are really in your front room and not in the cockpit of the plane. Time goes by and the processor speed of the PlayStation gets faster, the TV you are playing on doubles in size and the sound becomes surround sound. The effect is that the game becomes a lot more realistic and life-like and it is becoming harder to tell if you are in your front room or actually in a cockpit.

Then PlayStation release a helmet which US Air Force pilots wear in the F35 plane. It enables players to have 360° vision in any spectrum e.g. infra red.

It can be seen that as time is going by the *virtual reality* of the game is becoming closer and closer to the *reality* of actually flying the plane. It follows that at some point in the future the *virtual reality* of the game will be indistinguishable from flying the *real* plane.

This point of convergence of virtual reality and reality is the equivalent of when the observer and the observed become the same thing.

Imagine if the PlayStation produced a game of your life that was a multiplayer game. Other players around the world could play the game and you would see them on your screen at the intersection between their game and yours. This goes on everyday with games like 'Call of Duty'. Now visualise that the game was so realistic that you could not tell the difference between your life and the game.

So there is a point where the 'perception of' would feel exactly the same as doing it for 'real'. This is why Buddhists say that form is emptiness and emptiness is form.

It is like saying that the 'perception of' feels like something 'real' but is actually nothing and the experience of nothing can be any permutation of something.

The paradox of something and nothing existing at the same time is known as the co-existence of opposites and is talked about a lot in philosophy. In a nutshell this occurs because anything can be viewed from the two poles and by definition if you view from both poles you will have two opposite perceptions. So at the exact balance point where the two poles become one you will have the seemingly impossible coexistence of opposites.

So how does this affect my balance?

We have seen that the way we perceive reality may not be how it actually is. It is a kind of illusion of sorts. The relativity between the observer and the observed at the convergence point is zero, but it creates a picture that feels infinite, as if you were looking outwards from the pinhole camera hole in any direction.

If nothing really exists and everything is in our mind and consciousness the good news is that, if we adjust the way we think then we can tune in to what we want. This is what the meditation practitioners have been telling us for years, but did we take them seriously? Maybe we will now.

Imagine if you were able to navigate any observer/observed permutation like an iPod enables you to do for different songs. You would be able to do whatever you want! Your reality is a product of your thoughts and so it is within your control to find the balance required to enable you to navigate reality in a controlled way.

If reality is the experience of your 'self', that is to say everything around you is actually your 'other half' then it might be a good time to start treating your 'other half 'with love and affection to achieve balance!?

29 Acceptance – the Holy Grail of Balance

So far we have looked at several elements that constitute balance. Acceptance sits at the top table and is the holy grail of balance.

> *The ultimate destination of everyone's life is the acceptance of who they are, because once this happens everything else takes care of itself.*

Let us first define what acceptance means.

In any given moment acceptance is the receipt of what the moment offers without the need to judge, label, or change it in any way.

Acceptance does not mean that a person doesn't have a desire to change aspects of the universe, but it does mean that whatever happens or is received is accepted.

At the centre of everything is the acceptance of your 'self'. The degree to which you can accept events or others is by definition the degree to which you accept your 'self'.

So what does it mean to accept your 'self'?

At all times to be true to who you are, to your innermost uniqueness and beauty, without the need to impress others or fear their judgement. To trust your inner voice and become your own judge. To recognise that you are the best qualified person on the planet to just be your 'self'. To be real, authentic and to be at one with your true nature. To recognise that the universe needs you because you are a unique piece of the overall jigsaw puzzle and it cannot function without you. The universe will pay any price for you to be true to your 'self' and you need to recognise your own unlimited value.

So why do people find it hard to accept themselves?

There are of course many reasons. It is common for people to continually judge or have expectations of themselves in a way that is too harsh or impossible to fulfill.

In fact, the changes that they hope for in themselves can only start to take place when there is a greater acceptance of themselves. The acceptance means that the energy that was previously expended in the continual fight against the way things actually are can be used to make the changes.

In short, more progress is made with less effort. Many people are continually fighting the way things are at any given moment.

> *Controlling everything, perfectionism and creating everything in your own likeness is as destructive as it is constructive. Acceptance means the universe can co-create your reality in a mutually consensual way, which it was going to do anyway with or without your permission.*

The more you attempt to control the creation of your reality the less input you will have in it's creation. The best-case scenario is to be an equal partner and co-create your universe, the point of balance.

As we have discussed life is a continual sequence of cause and effect. Everything that we do will generate some feedback. It is important to listen to the feedback but if too much weight is put on what is said it can have the effect of undermining our confidence.

> *Feedback is important, but attaching too much emphasis to it will have the effect of reducing the acceptance of your 'self'.*

Often a lack of acceptance for your 'self' occurs when someone feels too fat, is concerned about some aspect of their appearance or cannot fit into the latest fashion. This is driven by the need to conform to what everyone else is doing. Many people feel uncomfortable if they are in some way different and standing out from the crowd. It is safer to be the same as everyone else. So who decides what being the same is, who sets the fashion?

Of course companies, advertisers and celebrities manipulate this by changing the fashion as often as possible, showing images that have been airbrushed, which are unattainable and wearing the latest sunglasses or clothes. The bottom line is that it is about exploiting people's need to conform to maximise the sales of products and make as much money as possible. How would you feel if you realised that people's lack of self-acceptance was cynically being abused to make profit and often with the most vulnerable group of people, namely teenage adolescents? As a result of this activity their 'self' acceptance becomes even lower.

> *Striving to be something you are not at the expense of who you actually are is a battle that will inflict damage, cannot be won and is ultimately futile. Acceptance of your 'self' is the only way to win the battle.*

As you accept your 'self' it is an inevitable consequence that you have a greater acceptance of others and the way things actually are.

If you imagine moving closer to a mirror then it is inevitable that your reflection moves closer to you. Acceptance works in the same way. The closer you are to accepting your 'self' then the closer you are to accepting everyone and everything else.

So what is the acceptance of others?

It simply means that you accept others in each moment for the way that they are and do not judge or attach labels to them. To share a common sense of humanity and respect as an equal without feeling inferior or superior to them.

So why don't people accept others?

It always comes down to a lack of 'self' acceptance. Egos, attachment to perceived power, fears, inferiority are all the usual suspects. If you see people treating others disrespectfully then you can guarantee there will be issues around alcohol, drugs, abuse of power and so on. The two things always go hand in hand. Anaesthetising themselves from reality will never solve the problem, which is that they have cut themselves off from their true nature. Like the inevitability of gravity, they will have no choice but to come back down to earth, often with a bump.

> *Treat others as you would want to be treated yourself because ultimately they are your 'self'.*

What is the acceptance of what is?

In each moment to receive the way things actually are without the need to judge, label or change them in anyway.

> *Each moment that we experience is exactly the way it is meant to be. The universe is as it is and this will always be the case. Your only choice is whether to accept it or to fight against it.*

Changing your perspective to accept things as they are is possible whilst trying to change the universe to how you want it to be, in any given moment, is impossible and exhausting.

If you listen to the lyrics of any love song, they could be about your relationship with everything around you, your universe and ultimate partner. Think of a pillion rider on the back of a motorcycle. When they go around a corner the natural reaction is to lean out of the corner, whereas for balance they need to be in harmony with the driver and lean in to the corner. Leaning in to the corner is counter intuitive but once fears are overcome it is the safest thing to do. The universe is the same. It is all about trusting it and feeling the union and harmony with it. This balance cannot be achieved by always fighting it or being afraid of it.

Achieving balance is the acceptance of your 'self', the acceptance of others and the acceptance of the way things actually are. In short, acceptance.

> *Is it time to stop playing 'tug of war' with the universe and start working together with it in harmony, as a trusted equal partner?*

Part Two:
Applying Balance to your Life

Contents

Part Two: Applying Balance to your Life

1 A Peaceful Mind is a Productive Mind

Beneath the stormy waves there is a quiet place where only you can go, a place of calm, of safety, a place to reflect, to observe but most of all to simply be.

Many of us start the day with a caffeine shot in our cappuccino, followed by the commute to work and a hectic schedule. Often the day is full on, juggling children, taxi runs to after-school clubs, work commitments and client socialising.

These activities all act as accelerants to the mind, making it run faster and faster.

If you think about a Formula One car going around a racetrack, it is doing one of two things, either accelerating or hard braking to get round safely.

Your mind is much the same, and yet modern lives create the acceleration but people tend to forget about the need for braking. To create the balance you need to do activities that slow and calm the mind as well as stimulating it.

For many of us a busy mind is whirring away without us even noticing it, it's just normal.

So, the first thing to do is to observe your mind in action.

Sit quietly and think of each passing thought as being like a cloud. Normally people attach themselves to each thought and experience the full emotions within it. This time you are going to simply observe the thoughts like passing clouds that come and go, without the emotion.

We are shaped by our thoughts; we become what we think. When the mind is pure, joy follows like a shadow that never leaves.

THE BUDDHA

Your mind is like one of those automatic tennis-ball serving machines that keeps firing tennis balls out. Each tennis ball could be a thought. When you observe your mind and your thoughts you will most likely find that it is running fast, like a runaway train.

The tennis ball machine can be switched off, but can you stop having thoughts? Try it.

Your mind behaves like a puppy dog. It can sit still for a moment and then it runs off again and has to always be brought back to the position of rest.

Practice observing and detaching yourself from your thoughts. Try to go say 10 seconds without a thought and then 20 seconds and so on until you can sit for a few minutes without any thoughts. It is harder than you might think.

Allow yourself a little time each day to slow your mind down.

It has the same effect as rebooting a computer; it just brings everything back down to earth so that your mind can work more efficiently.

> *Calmness in your mind leads to clarity of purpose,*
> *a clear sense of direction and a sense of oneness*
> *with your surrounding.*

Visualise a muddy pool, where you cannot see the bottom whilst there are ripples. When it settles then eventually you would be able to see the bottom. Calming your mind has the same effect, cutting out the background noise and enabling you to see and think clearly.

A busy mind is like being thrown around on the surface of the sea, with waves charged with emotion crashing all around. Imagine yourself withdrawing to a place a few metres under the surface where you can observe what is happening but where it is calm and peaceful.

Try this visualisation. Think of your place under the water as somewhere that you feel safe, maybe some fond memories from your childhood or from your family. Try and return to this place for a few minutes each day or when you feel stressed. It is relaxing to detach yourself from events so that you are simply observing them rather than living and feeling the emotions.

Some people say that they just do not have time to practice techniques to slow down their mind. The reality is that it takes a few minutes, it can be fitted in on the train or even just before you go to sleep, and the benefits of a greater sense of wellbeing and calmness are enormous.

Just try it! Have you ever seen a spiritual master who doesn't have a peaceful mind and who looks stressed?

> *A peaceful mind is a productive mind.*
> *Balance means controlling your thoughts rather*
> *than your thoughts controlling you.*

2 | Becoming more Efficient

Most people feel more balanced when they are achieving their 'to do' list in an efficient way. In order to manage this, you need to understand how your mind works.

One of the key components of balance is the conservation of energy. This means that mental energy should only be used when it is needed and if there are opportunities to save energy then these should be taken. The principle is no different from turning a few lights off at home to save electricity.

> *Don't waste mental energy or else you will pay the price. Always seek to conserve it at every opportunity.*

So how can you save mental energy?

Many people store their 'to do' list together with anxieties, worries and fears and other recurrent thoughts in their mind. This is intensive on mental energy because your mind has to keep going over and over the same thoughts to retain them, like a washing machine that is repeating the same cycle 24/7. Also, you always have the feeling you have forgotten something, and this creates additional anxiety.

The answer is to allow yourself half an hour to an hour each week to do a 'brain dump'. Quite literally to write every single thought that is in your head on a piece of paper or on the computer. You will find that once this is done you can relax your mind because you no longer need to retain your thoughts as they are on paper, in a trusted place.

You could write your list on a Friday afternoon and pick it up on a Monday. In between you could relax your mind over the weekend knowing that your list was ready for you on Monday.

Once you have a list of things to do you could arrange it in the order that you want to fulfill each task. The list now becomes an execution list.

On the Monday morning there is no thought required, it is simply a case

of working through the list.

Your 'to do' list basically involves three processes. Firstly 'What needs to be done?' Secondly 'In what order do the tasks need to be done?' and finally the actual execution of the various tasks.

The mind works the most efficiently when the three processes are separated and steps one and two are 'brain dumped' onto a piece of paper on a regular basis. This is the same principle as in a factory where tasks are split between different people for optimum efficiency.

There is a definite 'feel good' factor ticking tasks off an execution list. It just feels a lot more productive.

> *Writing a list of your thoughts every day means*
> *you get more done, you think about the things you*
> *want which attracts them to you, your mind can*
> *conserve its energy and you feel more relaxed.*

3 Practice Non-Judgement

Judging other people and other things is something that, if we are honest, we all do or have done. Indeed judging people is a necessary survival tool, so we can decide who our friends are or who we want to do business with. Somewhere down the line judgements will have been made as to their suitability.

> *Good judgement comes from experience. Experience comes from bad judgement.*
>
> JIM HORNING

So why practice non-judgement?

If you make a judgement about others, it has been derived from comparing them to a set of beliefs or viewpoints that you have. The first question to be asked is why do you assume that your viewpoint is correct and gives you the license to judge the other person?

As we have seen, we are all just looking at different things from different perspectives. There is no definitive right or wrong. This implies that no-one has the right to pass judgements.

Often judgements are based on stereotypes of different groups of people. If you think about it, these stereotypes often start as a sensationalised newspaper article and then they escalate, as judgements create a breeding ground for even more judgements.

The root of judgemental behaviour is usually someone's own fears or prejudices. But who do they fear? At the end of the day the person that they fear is themselves.

Judgemental behaviour is a result of feeling threatened by people who are different to the way you are. But let's think about this for a moment. If we were all the same wouldn't life be pretty boring? It is the diversity that gives life its quality and rich textures, so why not celebrate it?

Judgemental behaviour also arises from wealth and class viewpoints and

prejudice. The logic is that 'I have more money than you' and this gives me the right to judge you. This type of judgement leads to bad karma and is tantamount to shooting yourself in the foot.

A more realistic benchmark to compare people would be their values rather than their material possessions. Honesty, integrity and a sense of fairness are worth a lot more than any amount of money.

The first step to practising non-judgement is to go through a day and observe if you are judging people. I suspect that if you are honest that you are judging people more than you think.

The second step is to practise non-judgement by accepting people as they are and not for how you would like them to be. Remind yourself how boring life would be if we were all the same.

> *Unconditional Love for others is the love and*
> *acceptance of people for how they are, and not for*
> *how you want them to be.*

Being judgemental is a negative energy that will harm you. Conserve your mental energy by stepping down from being a judge and learning to just accept people and things as they are. What could be simpler?

4 Feedback is your Best Friend

Feedback is a two-way street, you can either give it or receive it. Both types of feedback are very important although they are sometimes undervalued.

Let's start with the feedback that you receive.

A common response would be to welcome feedback that reflected the recipient in a positive light, and to be critical of any person that gave feedback that was not so flattering.

This is exactly the wrong response!

Think of the feedback that you receive as being like the warning lights on the dashboard of your car. If the oil light was flashing in your car would you ignore it? Of course you wouldn't, because if you did your engine would break and it would cost you a lot of money to fix.

So why are you any different? If you receive negative feedback you should not automatically take it as criticism but instead listen carefully to what is being said and consider making changes to what you do to reflect this feedback.

If you react angrily to negative feedback it has the effect of making the person who is giving it think twice about giving you feedback going forward. This is exactly what you do not want to happen.

Feedback enables you to evolve, adapt and learn from your mistakes. Not all feedback is necessarily right, but always give yourself the option of at least listening to it.

> *Value feedback as a precious commodity. Make a habit of thanking people who are honest enough to give you feedback from the heart. Encourage people to give you feedback at all opportunities and never shoot the messenger.*

And then there is the feedback you give.

Your universe is made up of your thoughts. The Law of Attraction has told us that we attract what we think about. So it follows that it would be very useful to the universe to have some idea of what you like and what you don't like. Just like a hotel that asks for feedback so that it can improve the service, the universe works in much the same way.

During the course of your day, get into the habit of either saying or thinking 'I really like that' or 'I don't like that'. The universe will be very grateful for the feedback.

> *Just remember, giving feedback either verbally or through your thoughts enables the universe to better tailor itself to your needs.*

5 Balancing your Battery

I magine for a moment that your life is like a battery.

To find a sustainable equilibrium you need to balance discharging your battery with charging it.

Does this sound like a statement of the obvious?

Well, of course, it is, but in practice many people are not able to strike the balance and this can lead to problems.

The further you move off the path of balance, with respect to your battery, then the faster you will accelerate away from where you need to be.

So what does it mean to balance your battery?

In a nutshell living in a sustainable way is when you balance your own needs with the needs of everyone and everything else.

If your lifestyle is out of balance it will mean that over a period of time your battery will inevitably become more and more run down which will mean that you are less able to function normally and be able to fulfill your commitments. Short term fixes like 'energy drinks', alcohol, prescription drugs only act as a quick fix for the underlying problem and will cause more damage in the long run.

Sometimes you need to be more selfish to enable you to be more selfless.

So what should I do?

The first thing to do is to allow yourself some time to take a look at what is happening in your life. Look at all the things you do, including sleep, and write a plus or a minus next to them dependent on whether the activity charges or discharges your battery.

You should start to get a picture of what is going on. A common scenario for parents is that they find themselves fulfilling the needs of their children and the needs of work and partners and there is no time for their own needs, no 'me' time.

Well, there is time! There is the same amount of time for all of us in a day. The key is what you are doing with that time, this choice is yours.

Look at your timetable and be selfish in places so that you can recharge your battery. A small amount of recharging has a tremendous effect on your wellbeing. Sit in the bath with some candles, do an aerobics class, do whatever works for you and fit it into your routine. During this time others can sort their own needs out.

As well as recharging your battery you also need to implement

some strategies to reduce the rate at which your battery is discharging. Conserving your energy is vital to balance.

So how can you conserve energy?

We have discussed using the 'brain dump' method to empty your head and to allow you to relax your mind.

Another area where energy is expended is when you continually feel the need to convince others of your point of view. Conserve this energy because often people are not receptive to opinions and ideology that is at odds with their own. People tend to be transmitters as opposed to receivers. So let them be, don't vibrate air molecules unnecessarily.

Conserve the energy you spend judging others. Just let them be.

Conserve the energy you spend judging yourself. You are who you are. Accept it, because it will not change.

Conserve the energy you waste worrying what other people are going to do. They are going to do it anyway, with or without your blessing.

Conserve the energy you use to speculate what may happen in the future or dwelling on what happened in the past. The present moment is all you have. Simply focus on that. Why waste energy worrying about something you cannot control and that is going to happen anyway?

Focus your energy only on the things you can control, namely, your own actions.

> *Become aware of your battery. Conserve energy wherever possible, and always find time to charge your own battery. If this doesn't happen then the consequence is that you will not be able to meet either your own needs or those of others.*

Become aware of your battery. Seek to conserve energy whenever possible and find time to recharge it in your daily routine. Small changes now can avoid the inevitability of bigger problems going forward. You are not helping anyone around you if you are not first of all helping yourself.

6 Tuning in to the Moment

Our minds are programmed to only seek the information that we require to fulfill our various functions and tasks. The first time you do something you will absorb a lot of information and this will tend to diminish each subsequent time that you do the same thing.

This is good for brain efficiency but it means that the reality that you experience is a cut-down version of what is really happening. A bit like black and white image versus a colour image.

Have you ever had the experience of travelling to work and finding that, when you got there, you couldn't really remember anything about the journey? You were in autopilot mode and busy thinking about an important meeting or the sales figures from yesterday.

> *Do not dwell in the past, do not dream of the future, concentrate the mind on the present moment.*
>
> BUDDHA

The fact is that routine conspires to reduce our experience of the present moment. It could be that you were only sensing 10% of what was actually happening in each moment. This has the effect of making life feel dull and boring.

This is not good for balance because it means that you tend to live your life in your head, in a reality that is based on the past and on speculation about the future. Learning to be anchored in each moment has a number of benefits, which include a richer and fuller life experience and a grounding and calming effect which is good for balance.

So how do I tune in to the moment?

The first step is to become aware of when you are drifting into your thoughts.

The second step is to make a point of noticing different aspects of the moment you are in. It could be the expression on someone's face, it could be a cloud formation, it could be anything. Just make a point of noticing what you are experiencing. This will have the effect of increasing your present moment awareness and in time will become a good habit. Think of yourself as Sherlock Holmes, noticing things that others do not.

A greater present moment awareness will also make life feel fresher and more interesting and exciting.

One of the best ways to experience present moment awareness is to be surrounded by nature. Observe the colours of the flowers, the texture of the leaves and the reflection of the sunlight on the water. Try to take in 100% of the information in each moment. You will feel a sense of oneness, a sense of connection, a sense of being part of everything around you. Always make a point of noticing the trees and the flowers on your way to work. Just remember that whatever drama is happening at work, the trees are still standing regardless. It gives a good sense of perspective.

> *When senses you haven't used for a while focus on your present moment awareness, you will see everything in a completely different light.*

When thinking about the present moment, people often think of the visual aspect first. There are, of course, the other senses of touch, smell, sound and taste. These all join together to create the overall picture of each moment. Make a habit of using all your senses and, for example, notice different textures and different sounds.

The present moment is good for your balance because it improves the connection you have with everything around you, it is grounding, calming and it enables you to see your life from a different perspective that is fresh and exciting. Start tuning in to it!

7 | Life is Predictable – How do I overcome my Fear of changing it?

The universe is based on change and uncertainty. This simple fact is scary for many of us and, as a result, we try to create a safe haven in our life, a kind of bubble that is based around a predictable routine and framework.

Any changes that we make will carry some form of fear. Starting a new job or learning new skills will have an initial resistance, a kind of insecurity about whether we can do it or not.

As a result of this fear of change it means that people tend to live their lives within a predictable framework, a set routine. The longer someone lives within this predictable framework then the greater their fear of changing it and as a result it becomes a self-fulfilling prophecy.

Somewhere deep down, for most of us, there is desire to be curled up in a ball, in a safe and secure place like your mother's womb. The predictable life serves to fulfill this need and desire.

Security in life comes from evolution and adaptability.
Fear of change and a craving for predictability
simply anchor you to the insecurity you fear.

During the course of our lives we become more aware of who we are and of our needs and desires. This is an ever-evolving and changing set of goalposts. This means that the job that you are doing today may not be the right job for you in, say, a year's time. It is important to recognise that your needs change, so what you do with your time will also need to change and evolve. The fear of change will only hold you back and restrict your personal growth.

Your instincts will guide you on the
right path. Always listen to them and
confront the fears that conspire to stop
you being true to your inner self.

So how do I form a healthier relationship with change?

Achieving balance is finding a sustainable relationship between the predictability and unpredictability of your life.

As we have seen it is often the unpredictability element that is missing. It is this element that gives life its vibrancy and colour and the sense that when you wake up in the morning you don't know what is going to happen.

In the seventies an American psychiatrist, under the pen name of Luke Rhinehart, took the idea of introducing randomness and unpredictability into his life to new extreme levels. He wrote a book called *The Diceman* that follows his experiment to allow the dice to decide what he did in his life. He would choose six possible outcomes and then throw the dice to decide which one to do. This resulted in an entertaining series of events that charted some low points but ultimately created a success story with the formation of 'dice therapy' centres.

Although the idea of living by the dice attracted a cult following, it is probably not the best way to introduce randomness into your life!

Make a resolution to deliberately put something different into your schedule. It could be a workout class, learning a new skill, even just simply taking a different walk to work. Sometimes you may have a couple of options and could toss a coin to decide which one to take. These variations in your schedule and actions often prove to be the fertile ground for new inspirations, new openings and a greater insight into where you are in your life and where you want to go.

The limit of what is possible is the limit of what you think is possible. Living in a predictable framework has the effect of making you believe that living within the confines of that framework is the only thing that is possible. This can mean that someone metaphorically 'loses the will to live'.

Make a resolution to do different things, meet different people and introduce randomness into your life. Rediscover the vibrancy and excitement that is available in each and every moment. Trust your instincts to sense where the balance between structure and non-structure and predictability and non-predictability is for you.

8 How do I avoid experiencing my own Prejudice and Bias?

As we have seen, the universe acts like a mirror and what we experience is the reflection of our own prejudice and bias magnified several times.

So what causes our bias?

As with all things, there are many factors. Many have been learnt from other people and, of course, your parents are likely to be top of the list in terms of your influences. In short if they had bias or prejudice then you are likely to have picked up these viewpoints.

Bias and prejudice tend to proliferate in a positive feedback cycle. If you think about it, your friends tend to be people who have a similar outlook and opinions to you. That's why you like them in the first place. The more time you spend with them will tend to have the effect of reinforcing your shared points of view, which may or may not be biased.

There is an evolutionary principle.

> *One-eyed hedgehogs mix with one-eyed hedgehogs. You attract what you are.*

In nature, species tend to stick with their own for a very good reason. They have a greater chance of survival if they stick together. We are no different and there will always be a strength in numbers, but just be aware of the reinforcement of the shared viewpoint. Just because everyone agrees with something doesn't make it right.

Almost everything we do influences us, sometimes consciously and sometimes subconsciously. Think about the daily bombardment of information that you receive. There is the television, the newspaper, the music on your iPod, the subtle advertising campaigns, the books you read, the people you meet, the celebrity magazines, the list is endless.

You tend to buy a certain newspaper because the editorial viewpoint agrees with your views. The newspaper is carefully targetting itself at a particular profile of reader. So your newspaper of choice will always carry stories that reinforce your own viewpoint and bias. This is not good for your balance because if you were, say, cynical to start with then after years of reading that particular paper you are likely to be even more cynical. No newspaper names mentioned!

Advertisers are the masters at convincing you that you need to lose weight with their wonder food or you need a certain car to keep up with the Joneses. They are ruthlessly exploiting your bias. If you were balanced you wouldn't feel it necessary to dance to their tune.

So what is best way to avoid bias?

A balanced perspective is to love yourself, others and what is - unconditionally.

Firstly take a look at yourself in the mirror and be honest with yourself and ask the question 'Am I biased?' Becoming aware of yourself is the starting point for change.

Consider stopping reading newspapers altogether and using the time to read some books. Books will increase your personal growth whereas newspapers will reinforce your bias and in many cases reverse your growth.

Ignore adverts because they are designed to reinforce bias in order to extract your money. Do they care about you? Seek information from trusted sources not from people who would tell you anything to sell you something.

Remember that groups of people tend to reinforce their own shared bias. Seek friendships with people who approach life in a balanced and sustainable way.

> *A newspaper is designed to set your bias and viewpoints in concrete. This way you become a customer for life.*

9 The Wish List – What do you Want?

I am tired of this computer, I think I am going to sell it, it never does what I want but only what I tell it.

Does your life ever feel like that?

The universe works a bit like a SatNav. You tell it where you want to go and it will take you on the journey to that destination. The journey time varies from instantaneous to infinitely long and will be dependent on the degree to which you are fulfilling your unique potential or serving the universe.

So what happens in practice?

Many people forget to set the destination in the SatNav by creating a wish list, a list of what they want. As a result they tend to drift and never get to where they want to go.

So it is time to be clear to the universe and yourself by creating a wish list which details exactly what you want. Put it somewhere prominent and be sure to update it regularly. The wish list is not just material possessions but encompasses everything, including love, relationships, personal goals and so on.

The Law of Attraction states that you attract what you think about.

So a good starting point is to think about the
things you want in your life at every opportunity.

Some people create a visualisation board and draw or cut out pictures of what they want. The important thing is that you must believe your wish list is coming to you because if you don't then the universe won't either.

So do you know what you want?

Deciding on what you want in your life is actually a little harder than you might think. Many people make a big mistake by deciding want they want based on what they think is possible. As we have seen the limit of what is possible is the limit of what someone thinks is possible.

The starting point for your wish list should
always be that you believe anything is possible
and what you want should reflect that truth.

Share the list with your partner, or friends, talk about it, think about it, and update it when you think of new things. It will become clearer to you what matters to you and what doesn't and this may lead to different lifestyle choices.

The universe is a trusted friend, tell it where you
want to go and it will have no choice but to take
you there.

10 Connecting with the Infinite Supply of Universal Energy

The connection that we feel with the universe is like an aerial, it can be completely in tune, completely out of tune or anywhere in between.

If you think about your connection with the universe as being a bit like an electrical connection, then for many of us the connection has become rusty and as a result you are only experiencing a small part of the universal energy.

So why has your connection gone rusty?

It can be one of those things that progressively creeps up on you, often

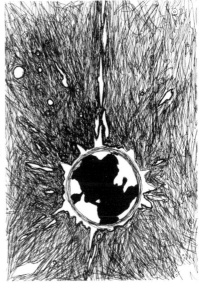

without you noticing. Effectively you are putting a barrier up between you and everything else around you. Everything else around you is simply your 'self' and so in effect you are creating barriers to experiencing your 'self' in a pure and unified way. The observer and the observed become separated by barriers in the process of observation.

In their iconic album The Wall, Pink Floyd famously portrayed a character who created a mental and emotional barrier between himself and the rest of the world, in order to create a stable emotional haven, away from everyone else. To a greater or lesser degree this is what many of us do.

Unfortunately cutting yourself off from universal energy is like a plant with no light or water, it cannot grow.

So how do we cut ourselves off from universal energy?

If you think of everyone on the planet as being part of you, then think to what degree you have a connection with them. If you treat people badly, with a lack of respect or with a sense of being superior or inferior, you will cut yourself off from universal energy.

A simple rule is to treat everyone and everything around you in the way you would like to be treated yourself, if the roles were reversed, namely, with respect. There are no exceptions to this rule.

> *Abusing a position of power or circumstance will simply have the effect of cutting you off from universal energy. The universe has a perfect accounting system and so there is nowhere to hide.*

Often the barriers you build are reinforced with alcohol or drugs, which give a temporary boost to compensate for the disconnection from universal energy but ultimately they make your connection even rustier. They act as a vicious circle.

How can we reconnect with universal energy?

It is necessary to take down the barriers that have formed over the years. Make a point of giving people you meet a small gift, it could be a small flower or simply a kind thought. When you pass people, smile at them and most of the time they will smile back. This will have the effect of creating connections, if only for a fleeting moment.

Your thoughts are just as powerful as your actions. This may sound a little strange, but as you are driving down the motorway send positive thoughts to all the people you pass or who are on the other carriageway. This works by creating good karma. You are connected to everyone and so take every opportunity to send them your best wishes and feelings, even if you do not know them.

Make a point of sending positive intentions to people. Touch the underside of your wrist when you want to send someone a message, anywhere in the universe.

You will feel the benefits by making a conscious decision to open up to others and by connecting to animals and nature. Go out of your way to make and feel this connection.

As you reconnect to universal energy you will feel the vibrancy and zest for life coming back, the sensing of loving life instead of enduring it.

> *Connecting to universal energy is loving and accepting yourself, connecting and empathising with others in your actions and thoughts, and balancing your pride with a sense of humility.*

11 Take a few moments for your Daily Appreciation

These days people tend to live life at a fast pace. Often the news and the media let us know about the bad news, the problems in the economy, the crime and lots of other stories which are doom and gloom.

People have finances to worry about, job insecurity and many other pressures.

Advertisers create desires within us to have the next product or fashion and in some cases cause a deep unhappiness within us about the things we do not have.

And there is the point, many of us spend our time worrying about all the things we don't have and forget to be grateful for all the things we do have.

Balance is not having what you want, it is about wanting what you have.

If you were to contemplate your reality, you would realise that the chances of you experiencing it at this moment are at best statistically very unlikely.

So it would make sense to try and enjoy it!

The first step is to build into your routine a minute before you go to sleep to think about the three things in your day that you are most grateful for. By thinking about those things it will serve to attract more of those things into your life. It will make you feel more balanced and content.

The next step is to take a few seconds to be grateful for three things during your day. It could be a beautiful sunset, meeting a new person or indeed anything that you appreciate.

Finally make a point of showing your appreciation for the people closest to you who can often get overlooked during the hectic routine of life.

In the big picture of life many people suffer from abject poverty and disease. Take a balanced perspective and appreciate your life and the lives of others at every opportunity. This will lead to a greater sense of balance and attract good energy to you. By appreciating what you have in your life you will open the doors to more of those things.

The best way to appreciate the things you have in your life is to imagine yourself without them.

12 Positivity and a Positive Mindset

Any sportsman or top athlete will talk about a positive mindset or getting in the zone to achieve success at the highest level.

Positivity or a positive mental attitude is at the foundation of every successful person.

> **I can is 100 times more powerful than IQ.**
> UNKNOWN

So are most people giving 100% positivity?

The honest answer to this question is that in many cases people are not giving their best in everything that they do.

Let's face it, the politics at work, stressful relationships, money worries all conspire to grow a more cynical approach to life, an approach where you don't always give your best.

There are others who try to cut corners by putting the minimum in and expecting the maximum out.

So what happens if you don't give your best – does it matter?

> **Whether you think you can or think you can't –**
> **You're right.**
> HENRY FORD

Effectively we all hold the keys to, and are the centre of our own universe. What you experience is determined by how you are experiencing it. If you think of the universe as being like an electricity grid, then you can consume electricity or put power back into the grid. As we have seen the universe has a perfect accounting system and so what you take out needs to be matched by what you put in.

What you are putting in to the grid is the degree to which you are fulfilling your unique potential. Positivity or a positive mental attitude is the single most important factor that determines your ability to serve the universe.

So, in a nutshell, in terms of achieving balance, if you have a low positivity it means that your contribution to the grid is low and so what you can take out is also low. To compensate for this people resort to chasing other things such as alcohol and drugs, which in turn make the contribution to the grid even lower. This acts as a vicious circle with positivity becoming progressively lower.

Let's be totally clear about this - if you approach life with a low positivity you are cheating yourself because you will never find the things you are really looking for, no matter how hard you look.

If you think you can have a low positivity and can slip under the radar you are wrong, there is nowhere to hide.

So take a look in the mirror and be honest with yourself, are you positive about everything you do and can you honestly say you always give your best?

If your positivity is low then it is time to consider making some changes. A positive mental attitude is the key to unlocking your universe.

122

13 Turning your Dreams into Reality

> *Dreams don't become their people, people become their dreams.*
>
> LOVE & MONEY

If you don't have any dreams then why get up in the morning? For many of us, our dreams have long been forgotten as the daily grind and drudge has taken over.

> ### You need dreams because they give you the spark, passion and desire for living.

Take a moment to think about your dreams and take yourself away from the here and now. Start to imagine every aspect of your dreams in greater detail and with a sense of them becoming real.

So how do I give my dreams the best chance of turning into reality?

Firstly, invest in yourself. The time that you invest in yourself is always the best investment you can ever make and will produce the greatest returns. The better you are then the better the chances of your dreams coming into fruition.

This may seem obvious but never give up on your dream. People often give up when they are close to realising their dream, sometimes without realising it.

> *Whatever you can do, or dream you can, begin it.*
> *Boldness has genius, power, and magic in it.*
>
> GOETHE

Have a plan. All businesses have a Business Plan which outlines goals and strategy for both the short term, say 6 months, and the medium term, say 5 years. So if you want to realise your dreams it would be a good idea to have a plan. It should set out your goals and targets over the next six months and also your medium-term objectives. The important thing about plans is that you check them every month to see how you are progressing and to make any changes to the plan in line with your current thinking.

> *Having a plan and checking progress regularly*
> *will greatly accelerate the transition of your*
> *dreams into reality.*

Create a dreams board on the wall. Either draw or cut out pictures to depict your dreams and spend a minute a day looking at the board and thinking about your dreams. The more you can clearly visualise and believe in your dreams then the faster they will become a reality.

Why are dreams important?

Think back to your childhood for a moment and try to remember the sense of wonderment that you had for the world around you. To a child everything is exciting and amazing and dreams are very vivid.

Now think to adulthood and in many cases the lack of excitement, the lack of wonderment and the onset of a cynical attitude towards dreams. The sense of life being in black and white, not colour.

> *Dreams provide us with colour in our lives,*
> *excitement and wonder and so it is very*
> *important to make them a part of our lives again,*
> *reconnecting with the inner child in all of us.*

14 Meditation – Taking Time to be a Passenger

Earlier, we discussed the difference between the engine driver and the passenger perspective of life and the need to understand and practice both viewpoints to achieve balance.

So what happens in practice?

The most common scenario for many of us is that we believe there simply is not the time in the day for meditation. The invention of mobile phones has meant that people are expected to be on call at all hours of the day and working hours seem to get longer and longer.

> *The connectivity of the modern world tricks us into believing that the universe cannot function without our continuous input, as an engine driver.*

For many the perception of meditation is of a Buddhist monk or maybe a spiritual master but in many ways it is something that is not relevant to them and even if it were, what is the point of it?

So what is the point of meditation?

> *When you have finished driving a car you switch the engine off. Meditation is a way of switching your mind off otherwise it has a habit of running continuously.*

If you imagine for a moment when your computer is about to crash then the remedy is to reboot it. Meditation has the same effect, it allows you to disengage from the universe for a period of time and simply be. Instead of having to control things and continually make things happen, you can simply be a passenger with nothing to do except observe and allow your mind to be empty of any thoughts. Meditation allows you to let the universe to go about its business without the need for you to interfere. When you realise that the universe can function without you then this can be very liberating.

There are many ways to meditate and many books on the subject and it would definitely be worth reading a few. A good technique is to focus your attention on your breath, to feel it coming in and going out, like the tide, and not to engage with any other thoughts. Simply focus on your breath.

Your mind is a perfect machine. You can choose to be its slave or its master. Meditation is the crossroads between freedom and captivity.

Meditation is not all about sitting in the back garden for an hour with crossed legs, although this is a very beneficial thing to do. Meditation can be incorporated into a working schedule in 15 minute slots during the course of the day. For example, it can be done whilst commuting or during a lunch break. The key is to simply clear your head, focus on your breathing and allow the universe to take all the decisions. Give yourself the time to meditate and switch off your mobile or any other potential distractions. These people can wait!

Another relaxing meditation is to sit in a warm bath with some lavender and some candles and dim the lights. Allow yourself this time to restore and recharge, you are worth it.

When you realise that meditation will relax your mind, enable you to lose the notion that the universe cannot function without your continuous input, improve your present moment awareness and increase your sense of oneness and wellbeing, then you will see the importance of taking a little time to practice it.

Sometimes less is more. Meditation will balance your mind and for a small time investment it will produce some significant benefits that will enable you to feel better and do more. Is it time to give it a try?

Meditation is about connecting to a higher part of yourself and understanding that all living things are connected to the same higher energy that you are.

15 | Food and Drink – Your Personal Chemistry Set

A familiar start to the day for many people is to queue up for a large cappuccino to give them the caffeine rush they crave. This is the time to accelerate in preparation for the demands of the busy day ahead at work.

At lunchtime, there is only time for some additive-laden junk food on the go, washed down with more strong coffee. On returning home a bottle of wine is consumed, which started out as being a few glasses, in keeping with the scenario on most evenings. This is wind-down time and the depressant qualities of the alcohol work perfectly. After a call from the project leader, a major document has to be presented to clients first thing the next day, so after drinking a can of 'energy drink' to stay awake the document is finally finished at one o'clock in the morning. The alarm clock goes off at 6.30am and the cycle starts again…

> *The food and drink that you consume is the fuel your brain runs on. You will never achieve balance if the fuel you put into your body is of poor quality, contains unhealthy additives or is simply a stimulant or a depressant.*

No matter how important you think a particular deal is at work, or a relationship problem or indeed anything else you can think of, the fact is that the person at the centre of everything is you. If you do not function then nothing else matters.

You are like a giant chemistry set and the thing that determines the composition of your chemistry set is simply the fuel you put into your body, namely the food you eat and the liquids you drink.

Earlier we discussed the impact of your brain chemistry on your perception. It can be seen that in some ways the way you perceive the world is in your own hands and is determined by how balanced what you eat and drink is in relation to the natural balance of your body.

Much is written about nutrition, but fundamentally rubbish in equals rubbish out.

The body of an average man is made up of around 40 litres of water which accounts for roughly 50-60% of the total body weight. The first point is that if you lose water through breathing and sweating and do not replace it, then this is going to impact your brain chemistry. You may have experienced this in the form of a headache whilst being dehydrated.

If you drink coffee or tea then the caffeine acts as a diuretic which will make you go to the toilet more often and as a result has the effect of dehydrating you.

You may recall putting litmus paper into a test tube in your school chemistry lesson to see if it turned red or blue. Red would indicate an acidic solution or low pH level and blue would indicate an alkaline solution or high pH level and pH 7 would be a neutral solution.

That was a long time ago. So how do pH levels affect you?

If you think about it you body is predominantly water and therefore the pH level of your blood and tissue is vital to the balance of your chemistry set and brain function. For many of us the food and drink we consume has the effect of creating an acidic or low pH blood composition. This is not good for us and fizzy drinks, caffeine and many processed foods we eat are very harmful in this respect. The acidity can create low mood and energy levels.

Refined sugars, which are present in a lot of things we eat and drink, have the effect of producing energy spikes which also affect brain chemistry by producing mood swings. After the spike there is an inevitable low which creates a craving for more sugary foods and a yoyo mood cycle is propagated.

Low mood levels cause people to comfort eat and, the more they comfort eat, the lower their mood. This creates another vicious circle.

There are of course many components relating to what you consume and how it affects you. Please be aware that what you eat and drink really matters to your balance, it is your personal chemistry set. The good news is that you control it.

> *If you had a car would you pour sand into the fuel tank or the engine? Of course you would not. Is it time to think more carefully about what you eat and drink?*

16 There are two sides to every Coin – Why not pick the Positive side?

Reality is based on two poles and because anything that happens to you can be viewed from either pole it means that anything can have completely opposite perspectives or anything in between. In a nutshell somebody's good could be your bad or one man's meat is another man's poison. There is no one way to look at something, only different ways of looking at the same thing.

Life is not black and white, it is simply different shades depending on how you choose to view it.

Understanding this simple principle opens up many possibilities to improve your overall balance. It means that you can choose how to look at things and that you do not have to be tied to a rigid framework of beliefs. You can choose to look at something in a number of different ways without having to choose one way to be right or wrong. Importantly when you interact with other people you have the flexibility to look at things from your perspective but also to understand and empathise with their perspective. By having a variable perspective, and understanding that one view is no more or less valid than any other, you are able to avoid conflict scenarios that occur when people have fixed perspectives. Let's be honest many people have the view that it is their way or no way.

So how do I apply a positive perspective to my life?

You love everyone on the planet but haven't quite realised it yet. So the first thing to do is to remove the hate perspective from your thought process and replace it with 0% love, as it is a lot more positive.

You love everyone on the planet somewhere between 0% love and 100% love and you can honestly say therefore that you love everyone. This is positive thinking.

Everything that happens to you is either showing you how to behave or how not to behave. The people who are showing you how not to behave are just as important to you as those who are role models. Otherwise how would you learn?

So you are driving along in your car and someone cuts in front of you. Previously you may have shouted a few choice words but now you say, 'thank you so much for teaching me how not to drive, I appreciate you taking the time to show me.'

Take the time to thank everyone for showing you how to behave or how not to behave. This is positive thinking.

For many of us, the actions of our parents are sometimes difficult to understand and this can lead to issues in later life. Our parents showed us how to behave and how not behave. They were not right all the time, because there is no right, there are only different ways of looking at things.

Thank your parents for teaching you what to do and what not to do. Don't waste your life trying to please them, just be yourself. It is their choice whether they accept you or not.

How you choose to look at things will determine what you attract into your life. Love will attract love, positive will attract positive, negative will attract negative and so on. So if you find yourself looking at something negatively then remember that you can flip it around and look at the same thing positively. This way you will avoid a whole load of negative stuff coming your way. Try it, it works!

Balance is not about what happens to you in your life – it is about what perspective you choose to view it from. There is always a positive way to view events, and when you select it, life becomes a lot more enjoyable.

17 Cut the ropes on the Guilt Hot Air Balloon

The universe is exactly as it is meant to be at any given moment in time. The only thing that you have control over are your own thoughts and actions. Whether you do or don't have control is a matter of perception, dependent on the engine driver or passenger view you take.

What you can say with complete certainty is that you do not have control over the actions of others.

For many of us, either consciously or subconsciously, we take responsibility for the actions of others in the form of guilt.

> *Think of your life as a parking lot. Others seek to transfer responsibility for their own actions by parking the blame in your car park. This is known as transference.*

Inevitably over the years the emotional baggage builds up and has the effect of slowing you down and taking you further away from the balance you are looking for.

It is not just the actions of others that can cause problems. The actions of the universe are fundamentally out of your control and therefore, in much the same way, it would be unreasonable to take responsibility for everything that happens.

The best you can hope for is to take responsibility for personally acting in a balanced 'win-win' way in any given moment.

So what should you do?

If you imagine yourself as a hot air balloon then the guilt, or taking responsibility, for the actions of the universe and other people are like the ropes and sandbags that stop your balloon from going upwards.

To allow the balloon to go upwards, to fulfill your potential and achieve balance, you need to remove the emotional baggage and the guilt that is weighing you down.

Inevitably some of the baggage will relate to your parents. You maybe didn't live up to their expectations, or there were some family politics or whatever.

The fact is, you did your best at the time, it was going to happen anyway, and they can look at events positively or negatively, just as you can. So there is no reason to feel guilty.

You would give your house a spring clean, so it is time to give your mind a spring clean? All emotional baggage and guilt can be thrown in the skip because you cannot take responsibility for the entire universe, or even, in some respects, for yourself, since you are part of the universe.

Going forward you need to visualise yourself as a piece of non-stick Teflon when it comes to emotional baggage. Let people take responsibility for themselves and put a sign up in your parking lot that says no emotional baggage is to be parked here. Become more aware of people laying the guilt trip.

When it comes to taking responsibility for actions it is everyone for themselves.

Not accepting emotional baggage does not mean that you do not care, it just means that you are not accepting responsibility for something that is out of your control, which will ultimately harm you.

Take a few moments each day to visualise yourself as a hot air balloon soaring into the air. Think about what colour it is and what shape it is. Imagine cutting any ropes weighing you down with a set of garden shears and feel your spirit rising as you unburden yourself of the guilt and emotional baggage.

18 | The Three Choices that apply to Everything

> *The consequences of today are determined by the thoughts and actions of the past. To change your future, alter your decisions today.*
>
> ANONYMOUS

Present moment awareness and acceptance are key elements of balance. As we have discussed, it is futile to fight against the way things actually are in any given moment.

> *You are a co-creator of your own reality and your thoughts and actions now are the paintbrush that shape tomorrow's canvas of your life.*

Your thoughts and actions at any given moment form the seeds of what happens to you in the future. The perceived time delay, from just thoughts to thoughts actually manifesting themselves, is determined by the degree to which you are being true to who you really are. It should be remembered that we are all divinity in disguise.

At any given moment, or for any situation you may encounter, there are three fundamental choices that you have.

The first choice is to accept things as they are.

You may be in a relationship and your partner is behaving in a way that you do not like or your parents may be interfering with the way you bring up your children. Whatever the situation, you have an option open to you to simply accept it as it is. If you try to get everything in your life to be exactly as you want it to be then you will never get to the finish line and as a result you will always be unhappy.

Life is a balance between accepting certain things you do not like and seeking to change other things to something you do like. Achieving balance is knowing where to draw the line.

134

The second choice is to take action to change things.

This is often the choice that people find hard to make, the path less travelled. In a relationship, for example, this might involve confronting your partner to effect change. To do this, the insecurities that your partner might leave you if you confront them, have to be overcome. The insecurities are fear-based and it is often the fear that stops people from taking the second choice, fear of what other people might think, of how they might react or a fear of any type of confrontation.

Tough love is often the best choice in the long run, but can be more difficult to deal with in the short term.

In a relationship, or with your children, if you have a fear of taking action to effect change, a fear of confrontation, or simply prefer to take the easier path of a quiet life, then those around you will sense this and exploit it, which will ultimately make your life a lot more difficult.

Never allow fear to hold you hostage when holding people to account. The chances are that if they leave they were not worth being with in the first place and if you try to 'people please' then they will never respect you.

If you allow someone to put a metaphorical gun to your head once without confronting them then they will continue to exploit your weakness at every opportunity in the future.

The third choice is to walk away from the situation.

If you decide that you do not want to accept a situation, and do not feel that you are able to change it, then you have the option to walk away, to take those things out of your life altogether.

Imagine for a moment that your life is like a garden. Walking away is like identifying the weeds in your garden and in effect removing them, by removing yourself. Accepting things is like appreciating the flowers and learning to like some plants that aren't necessarily your favourite. Changing things is like pruning some plants so that they grow in a different way going forward.

The three choices apply to everything in your life and knowing which one to choose at any given time is what decides your future.

> *Learn to balance the path of least resistance with the path of most resistance to lead the most fulfilling life. Walk away from any aspect of your life that instinctively you know will create negative karma, as this will multiply like a cancer.*

19 Nobody can upset you – You can only upset yourself

For many of us it is a normal everyday occurrence to feel upset because someone has acted in a way we don't like. Your partner in a relationship has turned up fifteen minutes late, or your children have misbehaved; there are many possible reasons to feel upset with someone.

These people have upset you by their actions and emotionally this makes you feel stressed and unhappy. If you think about it, these lows coupled with positive events during the day give your emotions a white-knuckle ride, which can often be exhausting.

Balance is achieved by taking total control of your emotions so that your feelings are independent of anyone else.

Since you are unable to control anybody else's actions then relying on them for your emotional stability is not a good idea. You are on a hiding to nothing.

The good news is that nobody can upset you, you can only make a conscious or subconscious choice to be upset yourself.

The fact is that all those years of being upset with other people needs to come to an end. It is no longer necessary to be upset dependent on what other people do, just simply decide yourself whether you want to be upset or not. So when a situation arises where you would have been upset just try not being upset! How does it feel?

No matter what anyone does, you always have a choice to be upset or not upset, or somewhere in between.

You may have deeply entrenched reflex or subconscious reactions to be upset at certain events but when you think about it the choice to be upset is always yours.

So what are the benefits of choosing not to be upset?

It enables you to be more controlled, rather than getting caught up in emotions and so your decision-making will improve. Additionally if you can keep your emotions more balanced then you will conserve energy, which is a key to a sense of wellbeing.

The same principle can be applied to other emotions. There is no need to feel disappointed with anyone in the future. Whatever happens was going to happen anyway and at any given moment you always have the choice to feel disappointed or not to feel disappointed. It is always your choice.

The colour of life is derived from the experience and the contrast of your emotions.

> *By taking control of how you feel, it doesn't preclude you from experiencing any emotions. It just means you can choose when you want to feel that way, rather than someone else making the choice.*

The next time you get upset with someone, say to yourself, 'I am making a choice to be upset – do I really want to make that choice?' A good visualisation is to think of yourself as a fish and each time you are upset you are taking the bait from someone.

Do you really want to be a fish in somebody else's keep-net?

If you always go for the bait emotionally, then other people will exploit this by pressing the buttons they know will cause a reaction. Children have been past masters at this since time began!

> *Balance is taking control of your emotional responses so that they are less dependent on external influences and more in tune with your internal compass.*

20 | Be Honest with yourself – Take a long hard look in the Mirror

There are many quick fix cures out there for all manner of problems. The fact is, though, that the only effective solutions will come about when you understand the problem.

The first step to achieving balance is to understand that the problem starts with you.

From experience, one of the hardest things for anyone to do is to take a good look at themselves in the mirror and to be truly honest about their faults. Some people cannot see them, others don't want to see them and some can see them but do not want to do anything about them.

It is not just the mirror that you can turn to for inspiration about your faults, there is always your partner or spouse! Often arguments occur because your partner points out your faults and you don't want to hear about them.

It's also human nature to blame someone else for your own failings.

80% of the solution is recognising the problem.

- So are you honest with yourself?
- When people point out your faults do you react angrily?
- Do you feel the need to spend your time defending your position?
- Do you listen to other people? Or do you simply broadcast your greatness without listening?
- Do you feel aloof to others? Do you feel beneath others?
- Do you feel the need for approval from others?
- Do you lack self-belief? Do you have too much self-belief?

These are all questions that you need to consider when you look in the mirror.

Remember that connecting with everyone and everything around you is a two-way process. It is not all about you and it is also not just about everyone else. Looking in the mirror helps you gauge where you are and what you need to do to strike a balance.

Being honest with yourself enables you to understand the problem, taking action to change bad habits creates the solution.

If you think about it, trying to impress people does not evolve your own knowledge. It is only when you start listening carefully to people, and observing what is happening around you that you start taking yourself to a higher level. If you notice, it is often the people who shout the loudest who have the least to offer. If someone is confident in their own ability, they do not need to shout about it.

To reach a higher level of awareness, make a point of listening to others, reading about people you wish to emulate, opening your mind to any form of honest feedback, including your own, and above all having the courage to make changes to your actions.

21 Give a little bit of yourself – Life is not just a Spectator Sport

A familiar pattern in this day and age is to go to work, come home, go to work and before you know it 10 years has gone by and you have never met the people who live next door, let alone participated in the community. You drop the children at the local cub pack but never ask yourself the question 'who is running the cub pack?'

Balance involves giving to others in the same measure as you benefit from their actions.

If we are honest, many of us are so caught up in the importance of our daily lives that we do not stop to think of all the people giving their time, often voluntarily, to improve the quality of other people's lives, including our own.

It may be that you or yours are a direct beneficiary of other people's contributions or it could be that a charity is there for you in your time of need at some point in the future.

Taking more out of the collective than you contribute as an individual is a short term win and a long term lose scenario.

Imagine a football match. It is as though many people are in the crowd saying this is wrong, this should be better but it never occurs to them that sometimes they need to get on the pitch, roll their sleeves up, and do a bit themselves.

Life is not just a spectator sport, it is also a participation sport and fulfilment involves striking a balance between the two.

Any volunteers will tell you that it is always the same people who put the most in, and as a rule of thumb, it is the people who put the least in who moan, complain and expect the most.

Although it is not immediately obvious, the law of karma conspires

against these people, as the universal accounting system is perfect. There is nowhere for them to hide.

So are you giving of yourself?

Giving to others in some form will have a number of benefits.

Firstly, you will receive 10x whatever it is you give. The universe works on a multiplier to encourage good behaviour.

Secondly, by giving, you feel the connection with others, the shared sense of humanity. This is connecting with your true self and will be uplifting for your spirits.

Thirdly, when you give, you will meet givers not takers and these are good people to surround yourself with.

Fourthly, although it might sound odd, when you are doing the right things, doors will open unexpectedly for you. It is what happens when you are on the path and you will instinctively feel it.

Giving of yourself doesn't have to mean giving every Tuesday night for the next year. Try to find something that is flexible where you can give an hour here or an hour there. The important thing is to give something of yourself.

> *Think for a moment of all the ways you benefit*
> *from other people helping you. Find the time,*
> *however small, to give something back. You will*
> *not regret it.*

22 | Detaching yourself from the Outcome

In every moment of every day there are outcomes or happenings. Your partner might be loving or unkind, your boss might praise you or overlook you in favour of someone else, the train might be late. There are many constituent elements to a typical day.

Detachment is a disciplined mental approach whereby you become emotionally detached from any of the outcomes during your day. It is as though you unattach yourself from the emotions that you previously hooked into, and choose to observe them as opposed to experience them.

> *Detachment helps balance by conserving emotional energy and allows clarity of thought through calmness and the consequent reduction in tension and fear.*

Detachment or 'no thought' is recognised in Buddhism as a key stepping stone to a higher state of awareness or perspective.

Detachment also relates to a disengagement from your own desires.

This means that you can disconnect your perception of your self-worth from whether you achieve certain goals you may set yourself, how you look, your success financially or achievements in your career.

Detachment means that irrespective of your aspiration, anything that happens or anyone you encounter, your own self-esteem remains the same.

Detachment shouldn't be confused with disengaging with everything and not caring.

In fact it means the exact opposite, because you become more controlled and more effective and have a greater ability to achieve your objectives.

> *Detachment just means that you have regained your emotional independence from situations where previously attachment to a person or an outcome had led to a form of dependency.*

In relationships, the restoration of your own emotional independence through detachment can also have benefits for your partner as the destructive forces caused by attachment diminish and they may also gain a greater sense of emotional independence. Dependency in a relationship should not be confused with love. Dependency is based on attachment whereas love is centred on detachment.

> *If you attach your emotions to outcomes that are outside your control then it is like determining your emotional wellbeing in a casino. Detachment allows you to put your emotional wellbeing in a place that is 100% within your control.*

23 Trust your instincts and listen to your Inner Compass

Within all of us, somewhere deep down, there is a flickering flame which is our innermost instinct. To visualise this instinct think of it as being like a lighthouse guiding your ship to where it needs to go and avoiding the rocks and pitfalls along the way. Your instincts will tell you whether you are on the right course or the wrong one.

> *Sometimes your heart tells you one thing and your head tells you something different. Often it is your heart that gets overruled.*

The problem is that in the chaotic world we live in, your instincts can be overrun by the louder voices of financial logic, fears, emotions and stress.

If you lose sight of your innermost instincts then inevitably you will end up on the wrong path.

No matter how much you ignore them, or even forget that they are there, your gut instincts are always there for you.

> *Your instincts should always be trusted, like a loyal servant that is always acting in your best interests.*

So how do I tune in my instincts?

When you take decisions always ask yourself the question, if no other constraints applied, what would you do? Listen carefully to the answer.

Use the various techniques to calm and declutter your mind, as this will enable you to reconnect with your instincts more effectively.

Be more sensitive to how things feel. If you are on the right path your instincts will tell you, as they will if you are on the wrong path.

Although your instincts are intangible, unlike your thoughts, which follow a logical sequence, they should carry a lot of weight in your decision-making.

Think of your instincts as an internal compass. They will tell you the direction to go but not the specifics of each step needed to get there.

Becoming more aware of your inner instincts is one thing, but being brave enough to act on them is another.

> *Fighting a battle with your instincts is ultimately one that you will lose. It is just a matter of time.*

It is like doing a job that you do not like because it makes financial sense to do so. Ultimately, no matter how much you fight it, the job will not work out. The same rules apply to a troublesome relationship. People often go through the cycle of poor decision-making several times before they realise that they should listen to and trust their instincts.

> *Finding the right path involves balancing your instincts, or internal compass, with your head, or external compass. Your instincts give you the direction and your head gives you the detail. When the two things come together you will know it.*

24 Focus on the People who Matter

As we have seen, many of the things we chase in life are very temporary and have no value.

> *All the things that once whet my appetite,*
> *Now bleed me dry, bleed me dry,*
> *Chasing rainbows and fireflies,*
> *To watch them fade away before my eyes.*
> *Love and Money*
> JOCELYN SQUARE

It seems to be part of the learning curve of life to expend a lot of energy in your twenties and thirties chasing after the wrong things that don't satisfy you, until the penny drops and you start to realise what really matters. And it is so simple!

> *People matter the most. Your partner, children,*
> *relations and friends bring the most happiness*
> *and stability into your life.*

- These are the people who pick up the pieces when life isn't going so well.
- They tell you how it is and not just what you want to hear.
- They provide sanctuary in a sometimes harsh world.
- And yet these are the very people that it is so easy to take for granted, like a piece of furniture.

> *Relationships are like flowers, they last longer*
> *when they are nurtured.*

Balance is fundamentally about your priorities. Relationships will only last if you invest your time in them. There will always be other things you could be doing. If you neglect your relationships then one day you may find that they are no longer there.

*There will always be another meeting but there
will not be another childhood for your children.*

Write down all the people who matter to you and ask yourself how much time you spend with them. This means quality time and not time spent trying to double up on the mobile to a work colleague. When you are with people always ensure that your full attention is with that person. Make a point of trying to contact people who you have not spoken to for a while, maybe one person a week for ten minutes, that's 52 in a year!

Touch the inside of your wrist and think of a person, the times you have spent together and send them warm intentions on your karmic connector.

Balance is built on the firm foundations of family and friends. Always prioritise those relationships above anything else.

True success is when your children leave home and you can hand on heart say that you have given them all the time and love you could.

*Do you need to re-evaluate your priorities? Trust
me, it will be the best thing you ever do.*

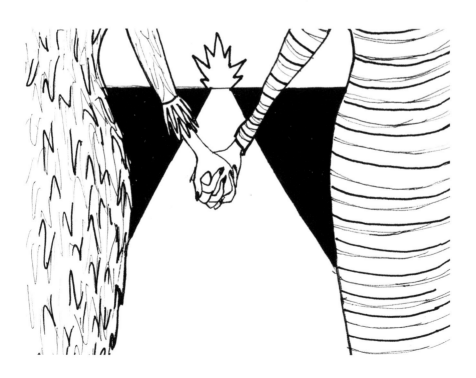

25 A Problem shared is a Problem halved

When you go for a massage you release the physical pressure points and the tensions in your body and feel much the better for it.

So why should your mental pressures be any different?

Sharing your thoughts and problems with people you care about will improve your balance.

> *Carrying the weight of the world on your shoulders is too much for anyone.*

In relationships it is sometimes difficult to share a problem because a partner or parent may choose to be defensive or argumentative when talking about the issue, and what started out as a sharing session ends up as a shouting match.

One method to solve this problem is the listening stone. Just find a stone and make the rule that whoever is holding the stone cannot be interrupted. This enables you to calmly say how you are feeling without the need to raise your voice, safe in the knowledge that you are being listened to.

> *Often it is not about solving the problem there and then but more about making people aware of how you feel.*

It has to be said that women are far more accomplished at sharing and listening. Men notoriously find it hard to be touchy feely with their problems as it may be perceived as a sign of weakness in the male world.

Day-to-day problems can be discussed more easily than issues that are deeper rooted such as childhood issues, low self esteem, trauma and so on. These issues, or pressure points, always act as drivers for destructive behaviours in your life. The destructive behaviours, for example alcohol, drugs, and relationship issues are merely the symptoms and not the cause.

It is only when you identify the pressure points and relieve the pressure that you can prevent the destructive behaviours. Always attack the cause, not the symptoms.

If you feel you have some issues then go and share them with a trained counsellor. There is no stigma, it is discreet, many people have issues just like you and the investment you make in yourself will really improve your balance and quality of life. Just do it.

If you allow problems, stresses and emotional issues to accumulate then the destructive impact on your life will also accumulate. Always share your problems and just be honest about how you feel.

Never fear how others will react to your feelings or allow those fears to stop you saying how you feel. It is your right to be honest about how you feel, and if others do not recognise that right, then you need to question the basis of the relationship.

26 Break the Habit of breaking Promises to yourself

It is a familiar story to see a completely full car park at the local health club in the first few weeks of January. People make New Year's resolutions to lose weight and get fit. A few weeks later and the car park is starting to empty again as people give up on the promises they have made to themselves.

> *Breaking promises to yourself is bad for your balance because deep down going forward you do not really believe in your ability to see anything through.*

So the best resolution you can make is to only make promises to yourself that you intend to keep.

How do you keep your promises to yourself?

Firstly, make sure that your promises represent smaller chunks of the overall problem. For example instead of saying you are going to lose 15 kg in weight and not seeing it through, set yourself the target to lose 5kg in weight and make sure you do see it through.

> *The best way to eat an elephant burger is one bite at a time.*

Secondly, recognise the importance of keeping promises to yourself. When you break them it is negative for your self-esteem and your sense of self-worth. It creates a negative spiral where you don't really believe you are going to see something through. When you don't, you are going to believe your promises even less going forward. Mentally focus on the fact that what you say you are going to do is what you actually do.

Finally, make a note of your promises and put them on the wall where you can see them. As you tick them off you will feel a great sense of achievement and this will boost your self-esteem.

As you get into the habit of keeping your promises to yourself you will feel a growing sense of confidence, safe in the knowledge that what you say will happen is actually going to happen.

> *A key component of balance is being able to trust yourself to keep your promises. After all, if you can't trust yourself, who can you trust?*

27 Recognising where you Are and how to Restore Balance

For most of us our daily lives consist of mood levels that swing gently from high to low. Some people have mood levels that are always constant, although this is very much the exception rather than the normal. When the mood level swings a long way upwards or downwards, or both, then this is known as a mental disorder such as depression, mania, bipolar and the like.

In the UK it is estimated that a staggering one in four people suffer from some kind of mental illness during the course of their lives.

The National Institute of Health provides a long list of mental health statistics for Americans. An estimated 26.2 percent of Americans aged 18 and older – about one in four adults – suffer from a diagnosable mental disorder in any given year.

The simple fact is that nearly all of us will experience some mental health issues or have close contact, be it a partner, relative or friend, with someone who does. So having a basic knowledge of how to maintain balance is important. Particularly when you realise that acting early and decisively either as a patient or a trusted carer can literally save lives.

Balance is about understanding where you are on the mood spectrum and what you need to do to get back to the balance or centre line.

The problem is that as a rule of thumb, if you veer off the balance line the natural instinct is to do all the things that take you even further away from the centre line. So if you are a little bit depressed you are likely to sleep too long, drink alcohol, isolate yourself and smoke cannabis. This will have the effect of sending you even lower in your mood level, which will propagate a vicious downward circle.

If you were to go on this cycle, then the further down your mood went the more detached from reality you would feel. As a consequence your ability to understand where your mood was and what to do about it would be greatly diminished.

It is the vicious circle of events that makes mental illness so terrifying and when the sufferer reaches pyschosis then, without intervention, the consequences can be fatal.

As you move away from the mood centreline then the rate at which you move away accelerates. So the further away you are from the centreline, the more vulnerable you become, because the rate at which your mood will change will be faster.

> *The key to dealing with mental health is to always keep the mood as close to the balance line as possible. If you can do this then the condition will become manageable.*

The best way to do this is to have two people who trust each other, one who suffers from mental health issues and one who is a trusted observer. They can give each other a score of where they see the sufferer's mood level between say 1 to 10 where 5 is normal, 1 is very depressed and 10 is manically high.

The person suffering from depression may score themselves 5 for normal, whereas the observer may score the sufferer as a 2 for being depressed.

This gives the sufferer a much-needed reality check. Often, the first time, the person with mental health issues may not listen to advice from others with respect to their mood levels. However, going forward they can learn to work with someone that they trust and realise the importance of having a second opinion on their mood level.

Instigating a system to more accurately gauge where the mood levels are is the first part of solving the problem.

The second part, is to have a list of things to do to return to the balance point. For someone who is feeling low this could be to do some exercise, sleep less, use a SAD light, no alcohol, see a medical practitioner and adjust medication and so on. Conversely if someone was on the high end of the mood spectrum the list might be sleep more, no stimulants such as caffeine, less stimulating work, adjust medication and so on.

Mood fluctuations affect all of us and it is a surprising number of us, 25% or so, that suffer from large mood swings. Prevention is better than cure. The highs and lows can be avoided by understanding where you are relative to the mood balance line, either on your own or with the help of a trusted accomplice, and having a pre-prepared list of things to do to get back to the balance point. Early intervention is always the best strategy to avoid large mood swings.

A stitch in time saves nine. This is the key to balance with respect to mood swings.

A lot of the problems associated with mental disorders can be greatly reduced by putting systems in place to firstly gauge someone's mood and secondly to intervene early with a list things to move the mood back to the balance line.

The majority of people do not have the large mood swings that constitute mental health issues. That said, they do experience mood swings or are naturally a little low or a little high. This can become more pronounced given the time of year when, typically, people feel a little lower in the winter months due to the lack of light. Try to gauge where you are on the mood spectrum and produce a little checklist of things you could do to restore balance.

Exercise is a great thing to do because the pain is very grounding and the endorphins your brain releases have the effect of lifting your spirits. If you're stressed at work, taking it out on a punchbag is also a great strategy.

Keep an eye on your sleeping habits, as sleep acts as one of the biggest mood regulators. Consider decreasing or increasing your sleep slightly depending on which way you want your mood to go.

If you can be honest with yourself, or listen to others, about your mood levels, and know what to do to change your mood, then it becomes a lot easier to achieve balance.

Conclusion

You have been taken on a journey through some of the main aspects of balance and given some practical advice on how to apply balance to your life.

So what have we discovered?

Firstly, that balance has a lot to do with perspective. It is the way that we perceive things that dictates our sense of wellbeing, the quality of our actions and the sustainability in our lives. It has been shown that the ability to have a variable perspective as opposed to a fixed perspective is key to achieving balance. Importantly, because balance is about how you look at things it is not dependent on what anyone or anything else is doing. This means that balance can be found within, and is not dependent on external factors and is therefore totally within your control.

Remember that, as reality consists of two poles, the observer and the observed, it means that anything can be viewed quite legitimately in completely opposite ways or anything in between. So if you tend to look at things as being either black or white, then it is time to be more flexible and remember the different shades.

Balance can be thought of as purifying the lens through which you view the world, with the ultimate aim of having a pure, undistorted experience of the way reality actually is. This coming together of observer and the observed is a special case where they merge into one, and hence the term oneness.

The irony is that this state of oneness is the natural state of the universe and when you 'tune in to it' you are merely tuning in to the way things already are. The universe is always balanced, you just need to realise that and experience it in this way.

The good news is that you do not have to wait for everyone else to find balance. If you find balance with the universe then by definition the universe will be in balance with you!

It also became apparent that changing your perspective to accept the universe as it actually is requires a lot less effort than changing the entire universe to how you want it to be. So investing time in yourself, to master acceptance, is the best thing you can do.

Just when you thought you were actually controlling your life it became apparent that the universe is the puppeteer and you are the puppet! This means that what happens is going to happen anyway and the choice is how much you enjoy the ride.

It turns out that everything in the universe is connected and you are not isolated and separated from everything else. Far from it, you are in fact an integral part of the whole universe. So much so that your unique potential is worth an infinite price, providing you are true to yourself and fulfill that potential and are prepared to ask for the price. Many of us undervalue ourselves.

To be as one with everything you need to lose any fears which fuel your ego. These fears have the effect of artificially separating you from everything else, giving you the sense of duality.

Far from fearing others you need to come to terms with the fact that you love everyone on the planet and they love you! You are in denial if you are not true to this notion. It is a positive mindset to love everyone somewhere between 0% and 100%, but at least you love everyone.

Time emerged as the most precious commodity, above money and possessions, and valuing it and using it wisely is always a good strategy. Time can appear to run fast or slow depending on whether you are absorbed in something or zoned out in a meditative state and you can therefore control how long you live for, or appear to live for, depending on what you do!

The universe has a perfect accounting system and the process of Karma ensures that what you give is what you get. So make a habit of giving whatever it is you want. If you want love, then give love. If you want money then give money. Just give whatever it is you want.

Balance is about viewing the universe as your partner, indeed as being an integral part of you.

Everything you do or think needs to be a win-win between your needs as an individual and the needs of everything around you. The universe cannot exist without you and you cannot exist without it, so it is time to work together.

The Law of Attraction identifies your thoughts as the primary currency of your universe and as such they behave like powerful magnets to shape your reality. In short, think about what you want and you will attract it into your life, and do not make the mistake of thinking about what you don't want!

When you have some things that you want in your life then remember to show some appreciation, as this will attract more of these things into your life.

Achieving balance is not something that happens overnight, but the process of improvement can always be started. It is something that anyone can do, with a little effort and the benefits will always far outweigh the effort.

You are fundamentally reclaiming what is already yours!

From my own experience, it is best to re-read some or all of this book from time to time, as the text may become more contextual to your current life experiences going forward. The book represents an ongoing journey through your life and should be a trusted companion over the years. Our respective journeys through life are all different, but the principles and rules that apply are the same for all of us.

Sustainability, collaboration, honesty, fairness, integrity, humility, community and service will ultimately always prevail.

Thank you for sharing this journey and I sincerely wish you all the best from the bottom of my heart.

Recommended Reading

The books below have been selected to help give you a more in depth knowledge of balance and how to apply it to your life. The books cover a wide range of topics and from my own experience, they had the greatest impact.

Seven Spiritual Laws of Success by Deepak Chopra

Loving What Is by Byron Katy

Making Time by Steve Taylor

Nudge by R Thaler & C Sustein

Who Moved my Cheese by Dr Spencer Johnson

The Miracle of Mindfulness by Thich Nhat Hanh

Mans Search for Meaning by Viktor Frankl

Path to Love by Deepak Chopra

The Road Less Travelled by M Scott Peck

Tuesdays with Morrie by Mitch Albom

The Power of Intention Learning to co-create your world your way by Dr. Wayne Dyer

The Power of Now by Eckhart Tolle

I'm OK, you're OK by Thomas Harris

Feel the fear and do it anyway by Susan Jeffers

Lateral thinking by Edward de Bono

The Secret by Rhonda Byrne

Think and Grow Rich by Napoleon Hill

Gut and Psychology Syndrome by Dr Natasha Campbell-McBride

About the Author

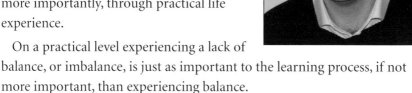

What qualifies someone to write a book on balance?

For me, it is the combination of studying the subject and additionally, and perhaps more importantly, through practical life experience.

On a practical level experiencing a lack of balance, or imbalance, is just as important to the learning process, if not more important, than experiencing balance.

It is like sailing a boat, you do not learn how to do it on a calm sea, it is only when a storm happens that you really learn how to sail.

Through no conscious choice of my own, my life has sailed through stormy waters experiencing what I would describe as extreme imbalance along the way.

At the tender age of 25 my meteoric rise and rise as a moneybroker was abruptly interrupted when my Porsche was swapped for a stay in the Priory Clinic.

I had just come back from New York with a new lucrative job and I went from stretch limos to a straightjacket, almost overnight.

Can you imagine being in that situation? Not really knowing or understanding what is happening to you? All your worst nightmares happening all at once?

At this point you find out who your friends are, who wants to help you and who just wants your money.

And do you know what? At this point you become passionate to find out what balance is all about, through sheer necessity if nothing else.

You meet other people in the Priory who are talented, gifted, sensitive and compassionate. Who are the crazy people, are they inside or outside? The dividing line becomes hazy.

The doctors told me that I had bipolar disorder. 'No, this is not possible because I am 100% normal' I thought. What is bipolar anyway? I later realised that it is the ability to oscillate between two poles of perception. It so happens that my ability to do this, my perceptive range, is greater than that of most people. Later, I also realised that it is not a disorder but rather a precious gift and a destructive force in equal measure.

Over the years, I returned to the Priory on many occasions and learnt what constitutes balance in the context of imbalance.

And what did I learn in those years? In a nutshell I learnt compassion, tolerance and above all a deep sense of humility and humanity.

My passion for balance was all consuming and I read hundreds of books on the subject.

And finally, I have been able to explain everything I have learnt along the way in a simple book, which will hopefully be helpful to someone out there. Oh, in hindsight, I would have loved to have read the book myself and applied the principles 25 years ago. Or would I? The journey has been as interesting as the destination.

The book came from my heart and I didn't want the publishers to edit it and re-edit it to make it more commercial. I just wanted it to be honest, authentic and 'real'.

And what became of me? I was fortunate to be able to retire from moneybroking at the grand old age of 34.

My wife has been an amazingly loyal support to me and through sheer determination we have been successful in business, despite some tough times along the way.

I teach and mentor now, to entrepreneurs, budding entrepreneurs and to people who are looking to fine tune their 'perceptive awareness'.

I have learnt that giving back is as important as taking out.

One of my relatives was Judy Fryd, who was the founder of Mencap, and a fierce campaigner for the rights of disadvantaged children. I admire what she achieved and hope one day to achieve even a fraction of what she did. I dedicate this book to her and all she stood for.

For further information about this book and an interactive forum for readers' thoughts, views, comments, ideas and questions please visit:

Website:
www.achieving–balance.co.uk

Social discussion:
www.facebook.com/achieving-balance
www.twitter.com/AchievesBalance

Alternatively the author would love to hear from you on:

allan.willis@achieving-balance.co.uk

Acknowledgements

Thanks are due to the publishers and copyright holders of the works listed below for brief quotations from the following songs: Lennon & McCartney, "The Long & Winding Road", "All You Need Is Love", published by Sony/ATV Music Publishing; Sting, "If you need somebody", published by EMI Music Publishing; The Eagles, "How Long", published by Warner/Chappell Music Inc; Justin Timberlake, "What Goes Around Comes Around", published by Universal Music Publishing Group/Warner/Chappell Music Inc; Dido, "Life for Rent", published by Warner/Chappell Music Inc; Love & Money, "Hallelujah Man", "Jocelyn Square", published by EMI Music Publishing; Peter M. Leschak, published by Pfeifer-Hamilton Publishers; Paul Williams, "Remember Your Essence", published by Entwhistle Books; Eckhart Tolle, published Penguin Books; Dr Wayne Dyer, published by Hay House; Deepak Chopra, published by New World Library/Amber-Allen Publishing; Jim Rohn, published by No Dream Too Big LLC; Mario Thomas, published by Hyperion; Brian Tracy, published by Vanguard Press; Anthony Robbins, published by Free Press; Anthony J D'Angelo, published by The Collegiate Empowerment Company; Georg C Lichtenberg, published by Nabu Press; Harvey Mackay, published by Portfolio Hardcover; Albert Einstein, copyright holders Princeton University Press and the Hebrew University of Jerusalem; Neil Armstrong; Malcolm Forbes; Jim Horning; Henry Ford; Bob Marley; Bob Dylan. Every effort has been made to contact the copyright holders of all material quoted. Should anything have been overlooked, please contact the publisher, who will seek to provide the appropriate acknowledgement without delay.